IS SHAKESPEARE
STILL OUR CONTEMPORARY?

Peter Brook and Jan Kott at the seminar.
(Photo Zeynep Oral)

The British section of the International Association of Theatre Critics would like to thank the British Council, the Department of Arts Policy and Management at City University, *Contemporary Review*, the French Institute, the Goethe Institute, the Polish Institute, Visiting Arts, and the Young Vic for their support and help in staging the public seminar on *Is Shakespeare Our Contemporary?*.

IS SHAKESPEARE
STILL OUR
CONTEMPORARY?

EDITED BY

JOHN ELSOM

WITH CONTRIBUTIONS FROM, IN ALPHABETICAL ORDER:

MARIANNE ACKERMAN, CAROLINE ALEXANDER, SHEILA ALLEN, ALEXANDER
ANIKST, GEORGES BANU, PETER VON BECKER, MICHAEL BILLINGTON,
MICHAEL BOGDANOV, PETER BROOK, TONY CHURCH, RUBY COHN, JEAN-
MICHEL DÉPRATS, STAVROS DOUFEXIS, GUY DUMUR, JOHN ELSOM, ALFRED
EMMETT, MARTIN ESSLIN, ANNA FÖLDES, ERICH FRIED, MICHAEL
HANDELSALTZ, DAVID HARE, IAN HERBERT, JAN KOTT, ELIJAH MOSHINSKY,
ZEYNEP ORAL, SUE PARRISH, HUGH QUARSHIE, KENNETH RICHARDS, TOBY
ROBERTSON, ERNST SCHUMACHER, YASUNARI TAKAHASHI, DAVID THACKER,
CARLOS TINDEMANS, RICHARD WILSON, ANDRZEJ ZUROWSKI.

BEING THE TRANSCRIBED AND EDITED PROCEEDINGS OF A PUBLIC SEMINAR
STAGED AT THE YOUNG VIC THEATRE, LONDON, BY THE INTERNATIONAL
ASSOCIATION OF THEATRE CRITICS.

ROUTLEDGE

LONDON AND NEW YORK
IN ASSOCIATION WITH THE INTERNATIONAL
ASSOCIATION OF THEATRE CRITICS

First published 1989
by Routledge
11 New Fetter Lane, London EC4P 4EE

Simultaneously published in the USA and Canada
by Routledge
29 West 35th Street, New York, NY 10001

Reprinted 1992, 1995

© 1989 The International Association of Theatre Critics
© 1989 Introduction and notes, John Elsom

Typeset in Garamond by Mayhew Typesetting
Printed and bound in Great Britain by Clays Ltd, St Ives plc

British Library Cataloguing in Publication Data
A catalogue record for this book is available from the British Library

Library of Congress Cataloguing in Publication Data
A catalogue record for this book is available from the Library of Congress

ISBN 0-415-04404-9

CONTENTS

INTRODUCTION

In 1961 Jan Kott, a professor of literature at the University of Warsaw, published a collection of critical essays which became best known under its English name, *Shakespeare Our Contemporary*.

The artist Feliks Topolski once warned me about Polish paradoxes, on the grounds that they are hard to translate, have many layers of meaning and Poles laugh at them. Kott's choice of the word 'contemporary' is an example. For two hundred years, from Gotthold Ephraim Lessing onwards, German critics had talked about the 'immortality' of Shakespeare, his eloquent handling of fundamental human themes which are supposed to change little from age to age. As a result, nineteenth-century productions stressed where Shakespeare generalizes and moralizes, rather than makes specific. In our time, these have come to be known dismissively as 'operatic' Shakespeares.

Kott took this argument to an extreme by suggesting that Shakespeare is *so* immortal that he's actually living next door, alive and well in cold-war Warsaw; and obviously, this was not so. There may have been bullies in Shakespeare's time, but they did not brandish nuclear weapons. But there was method to Kott's paradoxical madness. By slyly insisting that if Shakespeare is immortal, then he must be topical as well, Kott encouraged us to look at the similarities between Shakespeare's time and our own – or rather Kott's time then, for as Kott pointed out in the discussions which are the subject of this book, Shakespeare is more contemporary at some moments of history than in others.

1

Shakespeare Our Contemporary opened the floodgates to political metaphor. Connections tumbled through, some far-fetched, others closer to home. At a time when the rigours of Stalinist censorship could be felt through Eastern Europe, Shakespearian productions became a way of commenting on political events without running the risk of banning or imprisonment. Some plays, it is true, were discouraged by the authorities (such as *The Merchant of Venice* in the German Democratic Republic), but Ministries of Culture were reluctant to take arms against the work of a playwright so central to European drama. They would have made themselves look ridiculous.

And so Shakespeare did become a contemporary, able – by being dead and immortal – to comment on current events with a freedom that living writers could not hope to enjoy. Interpretations of Shakespeare's plays abruptly changed. In the old-fashioned, operatic productions of *Hamlet*, Fortinbras was often presented as the political saviour of Denmark, striding on in the last act to restore good order to the country after the débâcle at court. After Kott, he became the leader of the dark and menacing forces hovering on the borders of Denmark, waiting until the nation is too weak and divided to defend itself, a model for Polish history as the Poles see it. Hamlet was no blond hero, but the agent of national self-destruction. Claudius was no devil, but a strong leader weakened by guilt and self-doubt.

Similarly, Richard III limped around the stage under the weight not just of his humpback but of his Uncle Joe moustache. In other less politically explicit ways, Shakespeare challenged the East European orthodoxies of the time. Samuel Beckett, Eugène Ionesco and other writers associated with the Absurd were banned through most of the Eastern bloc, because they encouraged social pessimism. Ionesco himself would quote approvingly from *Macbeth*:

> Life's but a walking shadow; a poor player,
> That struts and frets his hour upon the stage,
> And then is heard no more: it is a tale
> Told by an idiot, full of sound and fury,
> Signifying nothing.
>
> (V.v.23)

Social pessimism could go no further.

Accordingly, King Lear and his fool became substitutes for the tramps in *Waiting for Godot* who were not allowed to loiter east of the Iron Curtain. At a time when we were earnestly discussing patterns of sexual behaviour, not wanting to be typecast, the gender confusions in Shakespeare's comedies, boys playing girls playing boys, helped to push the closet doors a little further ajar. What the *Shakespeare Our Contemporary* movement proved, if we were in any doubt, was that Shakespeare left behind a rich wardrobe of clothes, props and ideas which we could wear according to our moods and necessities; a liberating thought at a time of drab ideologies when Shakespeare had been elevated almost out of sight by German Romanticism, not just immortal but interminable.

The movement spread to the West. Kott's essay, 'King Lear or End Game', greatly impressed Peter Brook who in 1963 directed *King Lear* (with Paul Scofield) for the Royal Shakespeare Company, a production which toured Eastern Europe in 1964 and made such an impression that, as one Polish director said to me, 'we could not produce Shakespeare in the old way again, except', he ominously added, 'under duress'. Kott influenced Peter Hall's *Hamlet* with David Warner in 1965 and provided the central idea for the all-male *As You Like It* at the National Theatre in 1968.

In the West, however, the movement was aesthetic rather than political, if such a distinction can be made. In Britain, we did not lack contemporary writers who were ready to abuse the government, quite the reverse. Beckett and Ionesco were fashionable and, in the 1960s, the permissive society (whatever that meant) was in full swing. We did not need Shakespeare to say those things which we were prevented from speaking, but rather to confirm our new orthodoxies. It was also a matter of style. By bringing Shakespeare up to date, by making him sound more topical, relevant and accessible, we were trying to rescue his plays from doublet-and-hosiery and dress them up in more fashionable gear.

Thus, *The Taming of the Shrew* became a feminist play, with Katharine a freedom fighter rebelling against the marriage market, and with Petruchio as a male chauvinist pig who bullies her into submission. Why not? After all, the rough wooing is an entertainment to amuse Christopher Sly, the kind of drunken boor who gets kicked out of pubs. *The Tempest* became a tract against colonialism, with Caliban as an oppressed black. *Henry V* was not a hero king, not if you played him properly, and the tribunes were right all along in *Coriolanus*. The Duke in *Measure for Measure* can be turned into a greater hypocrite than Angelo, for he uses his power and position to force Isabella into marrying him, without even proposing to her properly first; while Cressida in *Troilus and Cressida* is not a flirt, but an honest girl struggling to survive among male war games.

These approaches are not necessarily wrong. Shakespeare is an elastic writer. He can be stretched in many directions before he snaps. Sometimes, by emphasizing this aspect of a play rather than that, a new perspective can be gained on the play as a whole, and often these varying stresses happen by accident, when there is a strong actor in what seems to be a minor role, or a weak one in a major. Nor can interpretation be avoided. Other ages have re-interpreted and usually simplified Shakespeare according to their own lights. Trying to prove that Shakespeare is our contemporary, however, became our kind of simplification, although there are many signs now that the mood has changed.

Kott has never lacked opponents and detractors. The Shakespearian scholar Helen Gardner called his theories an 'outrageous arrogance'; while Bertolt Brecht, whom Kott often quotes, insisted that Shakespeare should always be regarded as a man of his time, the product of a particular moment in history. His 'universality', if it can be called that, lay solely in the way in which he illustrates a phase in human development. Others have argued that Shakespeare is exciting precisely because he is *not* our contemporary, because his terms of reference are those of a first Elizabethan and not a second one, because he wrote in an English which is significantly different not only from other languages but also from modern English and because he startles us by his strangeness, not his topicality.

For actors and directors, these are not academic questions. From whichever direction they come, they have to ensure that audiences understand what is happening on the stage, are engaged in the events and moved by the outcomes. It simply isn't possible to have a revival of 'authentic' Shakespeares, as in music we have seen a trend towards playing Mozart and Haydn on authentic instruments. Every modern Shakespeare production is a balance between old and new; but to compromise in this way does not necessarily mean to reduce or to weaken. Sometimes recent experiences can add a new dimension, even a fresh urgency, to the original stories.

In 1988, for example, Claus Peymann invited the German-Jewish director Peter Zadek to stage *The Merchant of Venice* at the Burgtheater in Vienna, to coincide with the theatre's hundredth birthday. This harsh comedy is not taken lightly in Vienna. In 1943, Hitler's Minister for Enlightenment and Propaganda, Josef Goebbels, had ordered the Austrian matinée idol Werner Krauss to play Shylock as a way of inflaming hatred against the Jews. Peymann and Zadek were asking their Viennese audiences to contemplate the city's history of antisemitism; and Zadek brought the theme even more up to date by presenting Venice as a modern commercial city, where steel-and-glass skyscrapers mock the human dimension.

Shylock was played by the German actor Gert Voss, as a half-assimilated Jew. He wore no skull cap and his Jewishness expressed itself mainly through a self-deprecating irony. But he was an outsider among those tightly-knit family circles who controlled the Rialto. Zadek's target was not just racial prejudice, but right-wing capitalism in Europe, what is sometimes called 'the turning point' in Germany and 'Thatcherism' in Britain. It is a world where contracts count, to the last milligram of flesh, and blood too, if it is written into the small print; and where it does help to belong to a decent club.

Was this production a distortion of Shakespeare's original meaning, or an extension of it? Brecht would have argued that we cannot bury our knowledge of recent history or pretend that nothing has happened in the four hundred years which separate Shakespeare's time from our own. We have to develop Shakespeare's plays, if we are to perform them at all, in the light of our modern understanding of events which, in the case of the later Brecht, meant drawing out the Marxist morals. Marxism, however, is in direct conflict with many Elizabethan beliefs that Shakespeare expresses. Which view should we follow if we are producing Shakespeare?

In Britain, during the 1980s, there was a swing against Kott, who was sometimes treated as a sixties personality, very erudite and provocative, of course, but too subversive for his own, or anybody else's, good. Sir Peter Hall's last Shakespeare productions at the National Theatre were markedly more 'operatic' than those of his Kott-inspired days at the Royal Shakespeare Company. David Hare, who was directing *King Lear* at the National Theatre during the days of the conference, specifically rejected Kott's *End Game* interpretation. For Hare, as for Richard Wilson, Kott was close to being an old-fashioned pessimist. The underlying reason behind any assertion that Shakespeare could be our contemporary was that human nature itself did not change or progress, a counsel of despair.

Michael Bogdanov, on the other hand, finds Kott still a source of inspiration. These differences of opinion among British directors are reflected throughout Europe, often to a much greater degree. There are more radically modernized Shakespeares on the Continent from such directors as Peymann, Zadek and Mnouchkine than we would expect to find in Britain, and more trenchantly conservative ones as well. Nor is the debate limited to pro- and anti-Kott factions, or pro- and anti-Brecht. The contribution of oriental directors, particularly from Japan, is also significant; while if we were to select one school of thought characteristic of the late 1980s, it would be that of Post-Structuralism which influences even those who, like Alexander Anikst, claim not to understand what the term means.

As the translator Jean-Michel Déprats argued, we cannot ever pretend to know what Shakespeare originally meant, but we take the effort to try to understand him because this process itself is useful and illuminating. This lack of absolute

6

certainty is in the nature of language; and it applies as much to our physical contemporaries as to those who, like Shakespeare, died long ago but who left works which still attract and tantalize us.

The fact that Shakespeare's plays are performed more widely around the world, and more often, than those of any other dramatist, alive or dead, is itself a phenomenon as startling as the proposition that he could be our contemporary. If it could somehow be proved that one man's plays really had overcome the barriers of language, race, creed and custom, as well as time, if it could be demonstrated that the proclaimed 'universality' of Shakespeare was something more than a poetic licence on the part of his enthusiasts, then we might not have added much to the libraries of Shakespearian criticism, but we would have gained a valuable insight into the cultural software which drives our mental computers.

Such an assertion, of course, would have to be put forward with extreme caution. Is the *Hamlet* in Beijing the same as, or even remotely similar to, the ones offered in Paris, Stratford-upon-Avon or Moscow? Could Shakespeare be the inkblot in which many shapes can be seen but it remains an inkblot? Shakespeare, of course, had anticipated this question:

HAMLET: Do you see yonder cloud that's almost in shape of a camel?

POLONIUS: By th'mass, and 'tis like a camel indeed.

HAMLET: Methinks it is like a weasel.

POLONIUS: It is back'd like a weasel.

HAMLET: Or like a whale?

POLONIUS: Very like a whale.

HAMLET: Then I will come to my mother by and by. [Aside] They fool me to the top of my bent.

(III.ii.398)

Polonius is humouring the Prince, a powerful man at the Danish court; and, to extend this analogy, critics have argued that the presence of Shakespeare the Inkblot around the world can be attributed more to Western colonialism and other accidents of history than to anything 'universal' in his plays.

7

One purpose of this meeting was to consider how far words like 'universal' and 'contemporary' can be sensibly applied to Shakespeare's plays, using ourselves as test cases. It was as much about our perceptions of Shakespeare as about the canon or the man himself; and we did not seek to be theoretical in our approach. We wanted to balance the different insights of theatre practitioners, critics and audiences. The British section of the International Association of Theatre Critics (IATC) organized the conference, with help from the British Council, City University, Visiting Arts, Gresham College, the Goethe Institute, the French Institute and foreign governments, who paid for the travel costs of some of our contributors. Within our very limited means, we tried to ensure that many points of view were represented, from Eastern and Western Europe, from the United States and further afield, from Turkey, Israel, and Japan; and we chose somewhat polemically worded subjects, inviting controversy rather than bardolatry.

We were much helped by the intimacy of the two auditoriums at the Young Vic, by the support of the theatre's management and by the friendliness of our audiences. But perhaps our greatest debt of gratitude should go to those contributors for whom English was not their native language, but who none the less valiantly and effectively expressed their views, aided on occasions by others who acted as impromptu interpreters. Names and brief biographies of our eminent guests are listed elsewhere, as well as in the text; and it would be invidious for me to single out the particular interest of individual statements. I must, however, sadly record that two of our speakers, the poet and translator Erich Fried, and the Chairman of the Soviet Shakespeare Commission, Alexander Anikst, have subsequently died, within days of each other, in November and December 1988.

This meeting, however, was also a kind of birthday party, to celebrate the twenty-fifth anniversary of the publication of *Shakespeare Our Contemporary*, the most influential work of Shakespearian criticism of our time. We wanted to honour Jan Kott, who flew over with his wife Lidia for the event, and also in a friendly way to take him to task. As it turned out, we had something else to celebrate as well. For years, Kott had been *persona non grata* in Eastern Europe, for his theories had been so widely used to attack communist regimes. It was comforting to see delegates from the Soviet Union, Poland, Hungary, and the German Democratic Republic applauding the small ceremony in which Peter Brook donated an IATC birthday present to Kott, an early touch of *glasnost* on the South Bank. The plaque, incidentally, was donated by the Polish section of the IATC and thus came from a country which still denied Kott his entry visa.

In editing the transcriptions, I have often shortened the speeches but tried to maintain the flow of conversation and argument; and I have added some paragraphs at the start of each chapter to describe why we chose the subject in the first place. I have also separated typographically the set speeches from the conversations which followed and I must apologize to those knowledgeable contributors from the audience whose names were not known to me.

One final word about the IATC, which is a UNESCO organization which seeks 'to further the knowledge and appreciation of the world's theatre, and to promote cultural understanding among theatre writers of all nations'. There are some 2500 members of the IATC in thirty-five countries around the world. Frankly, an international association which tries to make the world a better place for theatre critics is not always treated with the respect it deserves, particularly in Britain, which is no longer a member of UNESCO. I can understand such scepticism without subscribing to it. A former Swedish Minister for Education and the Arts, Jan-Eric Wikstrom, once told me that in his view most economic and political problems at an international level were, at root, cultural questions. They started with verbal misunderstandings, which nobody had bothered to analyse, and proceeded, when all the other cultural differences were taken into account, towards a total muddle of ends and means.

The IATC exists to sort through these cultural confusions, in as much as they are expressed through the performing arts. The extent to which we can or cannot do so is perhaps best illustrated by the proceedings recorded in this book, which readers are in a better position than I to judge.

SESSION 1

IS SHAKESPEARE STILL OUR CONTEMPORARY?

with Michael Bogdanov, Guy Dumur,
Erich Fried, Jan Kott, David Thacker
and, in the chair, Martin Esslin

Our first discussion took place in the Young Vic's main theatre. The intention was to give Professor Kott a chance to recant before facing the wrath of the Shakespearian purists, either the traditionalists or those who, like Brecht, believed that Shakespeare could only be appreciated within a modern historical perspective.

In the chair was Martin Esslin, a Hungarian by birth, who had emigrated to Britain before the Second World War and joined the BBC. He became Head of BBC Radio Drama, and after his retirement from the BBC in 1977, had become Professor of Drama at Stanford University in California. In addition to translating many English plays into German, he has published several books of theatre criticism, including *The Theatre of the Absurd* and *Brecht: A Choice of Evils*.

The scene itself was somewhat like a tribunal. On the forestage were six chairs for the main speakers, while behind them on the main stage sat two rows of theatre critics from various countries, like an unofficial jury. Confronting them were the members of the audience, who drifted in slowly to the semicircular rows of seating and took out their notebooks and pencils, the critics of the critics. One chair was empty on the forestage. Erich Fried's plane had been delayed by fog at Frankfurt airport; and nobody knew when or whether he could arrive.

Esslin began by asking the direct question, 'Is Shakespeare still our contemporary?'; and Professor Kott leant forward towards the microphone, clutching a bunch of what looked like indecipherable notes. He spoke softly with a Polish accent that living in America has not encouraged him to discard.

*

JAN KOTT: I want to begin by describing a little incident, a scene, if you like, from the late 1850s. The setting is Jersey, in the Channel Islands. Two men are walking by the sea on a winter's evening. One is an old man and the other is his son. The young man asks the older, 'Father, what do you think of this exile?' and the old man says, 'It will take a long time.'

Silence.

After a minute or so, the young man asks, 'Father, what are you going to do?' The father answers, 'I shall watch the ocean.' After a moment, the old man asks the younger, 'And what will you do?' His son replies, 'I shall translate Shakespeare.'

The old man was, of course, Victor Hugo and his son became one of the first French translators of Shakespeare. This little incident helps to answer the question. While Shakespeare is nearly always in one sense or another our contemporary, there are times when, to paraphrase George Orwell, he is more contemporary than at others.

Shakespeare was, of course, Victor Hugo's contemporary, but even within this story, there are two different time perspectives. There is, on the one hand, the ocean, the time-lessness of the seas, which washed the Jersey shores as they did the beaches below Beachy Head in *King Lear*. But there is also the specific time of exile. Victor Hugo was sent into exile by Napoleon le Petit in 1855 and stayed in the Channel Islands until 1870; and during this time of exile, Shakespeare was his contemporary, *their* contemporary, whose words seemed to comment directly on what they were enduring then.

This was not Victor Hugo's first acquaintance with Shakespeare. I need hardly mention his Preface to *Cromwell* (1827), which appeared a few years before the great Romantic spectacle of *Hernani* (1830). What was the issue here? That history does not behave as Neo-Classical tragedies would lead us to suspect. History is disgusting. It has a bad smell. But how could they, who had been brought up on Racine, tolerate on a tragic stage, kings who cursed like coachmen and queens who behaved like fishwives? The impact of Shakespeare for the whole Romantic period was

11

very strong. For Victor Hugo's generation, and those who were a little bit younger than him, the choice was between Racine, who was not their contemporary, and Shakespeare, who was.

But what do we mean here by 'contemporary'? I think it's obvious. It is some kind of relationship between two times, one on the stage and the other off it. One is the time inhabited by the actors, the other is the time inhabited by the audience. The relationship between those two times is what finally establishes whether Shakespeare is considered to be a contemporary or not. When the two times are closely connected, then Shakespeare is our contemporary.

Let me quote from Hamlet's speech to Polonius about the actors. 'Let them be well-used, for they are the abstract and brief chronicles of the time.' The most important word here is *time*. What time? Shakespeare was the personal contemporary of his audiences at the Globe and Blackfriars, not so far from here. He was, for the first time, a contemporary, because he was living at the same time. He shopped in the same market place as his audiences shopped. He wrote his plays for audiences from that market place. He shared their images of the city, the carnivals and the folk lore. That is the first and primary sense in which Shakespeare was a contemporary.

But when we use this interesting little cliché, Shakespeare our contemporary, we do not mean it in this sense. We mean that Shakespeare has become a contemporary to our changing times and that these times have affected our perception of Shakespeare. Everybody knows that Victor Hugo influenced all the other Romantics in his attachment to Shakespeare, but Shakespeare was also influenced by Hugo and his generation. Shakespeare has always been influenced by those who interpret him, from Hugo to Brecht and Beckett. We have a kind of double dialectical relationship – the changing times and the changing images of Shakespeare.

Perhaps the best way to appreciate this changing image of Shakespeare and Shakespearian characters is to take two very well-known quotations, from Goethe and from Brecht. The first comes from *Wilhelm Meisters Lehrjahre*, where Goethe writes about Hamlet like this: 'A beautiful, pure, noble, highly moral being without the strength of nerve that makes a hero, founders under a burden which he can neither carry nor throw off. All duties are holy for him, but the present one is too heavy.' The most important word here is the *present*.

What was then the present? The year was 1795, three years after the execution of the French King, Louis XVI, one or two years after the execution of Danton, one year after the execution of Robespierre. That was the time in France. What about Germany? In Germany, the time is of one or two hundred little kingdoms, many courts. The idealistic young men of Germany at that time were not of Goethe's generation, who was forty-seven, but of Kleist's, Heinrich von Kleist, whose great historical drama, *Prinz Friedrich von Homburg*, was published some ten to fifteen years after my quotation from Goethe. The prince was also a dreamer, unsure of himself, like Hamlet a psychological study. On French theatrical posters in the provinces, Hamlet used to be billed as 'distrait', distracted, absent-minded! A characteristic shared by Prinz Friedrich von Homburg. From Goethe onwards, for the generations which immediately succeeded him, Hamlet was portrayed as a noble soul, too weak to tackle the problems of his time. That was their contemporary vision.

Brecht had a different perspective. In *Kleines Organon für das Theater* (1949), written just after the war, he described *Hamlet* like this: 'The theatre should always be mindful of the needs of its time. Let us take, as an example, the old play of *Hamlet*. I believe that in the view of these bloody and gloomy times. . . .' It's always time! Time! The time to be contemporary, the time to start the dialogue, the understanding, the time of Shakespeare and the time of reading Shakespeare, our time, your time, Shakespeare's time! '. . . bloody and gloomy times in which I am writing, in view of the criminal ruling classes and the general despair, the story of the play might read like this.' Brecht points out that it is a time of war and Fortinbras is starting another war, against Poland. Hamlet meets young Fortinbras while he is marching with his troops. It is the first time in Shakespeare that Poland is mentioned; and we rarely bother

13

to talk about Poland when discussing *Hamlet*, but for Brecht in 1949, Poland was a central place, and connected with the time of *Hamlet* and his writings on *Hamlet*. 'Overcome by this warrior-like example of Fortinbras, Hamlet turns back and with a piece of barbaric butchery, slaughters his uncle, his mother and himself, leaving Denmark to the Norwegians.'

'Leaving Denmark to the Norwegians'! That's a strange summary of the plot of *Hamlet*. But that was Brecht's perspective after the Second World War, leaving territory to the occupation, to the king and a different king. 'That having happened, the young man Hamlet has made a most ineffectual use of his powers of reasoning. Faced by the irrational, his reasoning becomes totally impractical. He falls a tragic victim to the discrepancy between such reasoning and such action.'

It is astonishing that we are not perhaps after all so very far from Goethe. There is a similar kind of split, which in Goethe is primarily a division in his character. In Brecht, there is a split in ideology, or finally a split between past and present. For Brecht's Hamlet, the present is too difficult, just as the present was too difficult for Goethe's Hamlet.

This kind of opposition, the inner split, seems to me in some way represented by the contrast between Wittenberg and Elsinore, or between, in Brecht's term, the old habits and the new enlightenment of Wittenberg. Wittenberg is a university centre, a place for art, historical research and the humanities. But Elsinore is bloody and feudal. But where is the audience living, in Wittenberg or Elsinore? Goethe looked at Elsinore through the perspective of his Wittenberg–Weimar. But Brecht did not. For a director of *Hamlet*, this is one of the most important questions. Is the audience *inside* the prison of Elsinore, or are they outside? For Goethe, the most contemporary character in *Hamlet* was young Hamlet. For Brecht in 1949, it was Fortinbras. That was the difference.

One last example. A few years ago, I was in Dubrovnik, which is a Renaissance city and a beautiful beach resort on the Mediterranean. They have a festival there during the summer, where there are many performances. People drink, dance, make love – and go to the theatre. There is also a castle, where they often perform *Hamlet*; and in one production I saw there, Claudius's court were dressed in modern costumes. They looked like the people from the beach. Into this pleasant society, there suddenly comes a ghost, saying, 'Revenge, Hamlet, revenge!'

Revenge what? The holocaust? Stalin's time? Hitler's time? The ghost was quite ridiculous. I didn't know what the director was trying to do. The meaning of the play was completely reversed. We were living in Dubrovnik, where Elsinore was a long way off, a thing of the past, the feudal past. Even the holocaust belonged to history. The present was the beach, and making love, and drinking wine. The ghost was something different, the ghost of an old idea perhaps, an old ideology, an ancient story.

This seems to me the crucial point. It demonstrates how Shakespeare could have been our contemporary twenty-five years ago, whereas he is not so much of a contemporary today. During the last ten years, our understanding of Shakespeare has changed. In some ways, I feel like a ghost myself. Twenty-five years is a long time. In one Shakespearian production in Britain during the 1970s, the ghost came on in a military uniform from the First World War! That was how far off the call for revenge seemed then!

But the Shakespeare of twenty-five years ago was my contemporary in a different way. He was also the contemporary of the relatively young Peter Hall, and the relatively young Peter Brook, and Kenneth Tynan, and Martin Esslin. We could see that contemporary quality not only in *Hamlet* but also in the complex ambiguities of sexual relationships in Shakespeare's plays, Shakespeare seen through the eyes of Jean Genet and Genet seen through the eyes of Shakespeare. We could play Shakespeare simply and directly because he meant a lot to us. But that was a long time ago, and even leaving behind my metaphor of the opposition between Wittenberg and Elsinore, I would like to stress that plays *have* to be seen within some definite context, some specific time, some specific place.

It often seems to me that nowadays Shakespeare is placed in no time and in no particular place. I have a great

15

admiration for Ariane Mnouchkine, but when I watch her Shakespearian productions with big Japanese-type dolls and Samurais and a kind of mock Kabuki, I think to myself, 'This is fake Japanese and fake Shakespeare.' It is quite different from actual Shakespearian productions in Japan, the exact opposite of the work of Kurosawa, whose films you may know, *The Throne in Blood* or *Ran*, which means 'amok', or fury, or madness. Kurosawa has found a new historical place for Shakespeare. What is contemporary in Shakespeare for Kurosawa is terror, the terror of *King Lear* and the terror of *The Throne in Blood*. Kurosawa's *Lear* is like the *King Lear* of Peter Brook, timeless but contemporary. The one Shakespeare who is not our contemporary is the Shakespeare of nowhere and no time.

The British director, Michael Bogdanov, spoke next. Bogdanov belongs to that generation of directors which succeeded Peter Hall and Peter Brook at the Royal Shakespeare Company in the late 1960s. He was an assistant director to Brook's *A Midsummer Night's Dream* (1970). His RSC productions included *Bartholomew Fair* and *The Taming of the Shrew*; and he became an Associate Director at the National Theatre, where he directed Howard Brenton's controversial play, *The Romans in Britain* (1980). With the actor Michael Pennington, he started the English Shakespeare Company in May 1986; and in 1989 he was appointed to succeed Peter Zadek as the artistic director of the Schauspielhaus in Hamburg, a rare honour for a British director.

Bogdanov began by paying tribute to Kott, Esslin and Peter Brook as the three formative influences on his directing career, those from whom 'all my thinking of the past ten, twelve years springs'.

MICHAEL BOGDANOV: What saddens me is that we have to discuss this question at all. As a practitioner I have to create the bridge that Jan Kott has talked about, between the stage and the market place. I can only make that relationship actual if I understand, first of all, what is happening in the streets. I look for my inspiration for the day's rehearsal, and for what the plays mean, in the headlines of the papers. I have only myself to blame or to credit for the interpretation of the text. There is nobody else. When I read a play, I only understand it one way. It's no use anybody telling me that somebody else thinks about it like this or that someone in the audience knows the play backwards and thinks something else.

16

Shakespeare's dead. It's hard enough, even when you've got a living writer sitting by your side to know exactly what that writer means and quite often if you say to a writer when you're working on his new play, 'What do you mean by that?', he will say something and you will answer, 'But, hang on! You can't mean that because of what you've said in another scene!' And the writer will say, 'Oh yes, you're right! I'd better change it.' It's hard enough if you have the writer beside you and it's harder if the writer's at the end of a telephone, and it's harder still if you can't contact the writer at all. And if the writer's been dead for four hundred years . . .!

The problem is that unless plays are accessible, they don't live in anybody's minds or futures. For me, the principal aim of the theatre is not just to illuminate and become the brief chronicle of the time. It is also to aid the process of social change. Art for me at its highest point is an instrument of social change. Often in the vanguard of revolution are the artists who are articulating the thoughts, ideas and theories of the period. It is no accident that some of the best theatre writing today has come from Ireland, and has done for the past ten years. The political, social and religious circumstances have created the impetus for people to articulate their feelings about this situation. Poets, playwrights, sculptors and short-story writers see the other side of the social coin, the violence, the brutality.

And so, when I walk into a rehearsal with my group in *Henry IV* and *Henry V*, I look for the way in which the political circumstances were handled then, and find inspirational parallels in what is happening now. We governed disgustingly in the fourteenth century and we are still governing disgustingly today. When Prince John of Lancaster meets the Archbishop on neutral ground, and tricks the rebels into laying down their arms, I think of Reagan and Gorbachev in Reykjavik. The inspiration for that day is an incident which has just occurred and which sets up resonances to create a link between the play, the ideas that are expressed through it and the contemporary audience that will eventually receive it.

It follows that if one is using the contemporary political

scene for one's inspiration, then it must link up with a political past that was once contemporary too. The forging of that link is of absolute importance. It is in the nature of Shakespeare to analyse power, what makes brother kill brother and mother betray son, father fight son and cousin kill cousin in the name of what is laughably called 'divine right', which ends up as nothing more than the crock of gold at the top of the pyramid. What makes us continue to try to achieve these things in the name of humanity? Why is power such an absolute, such a corrupting force?

These ideas don't find much currency in this country where historically we have been apolitical in our approach to the arts and the theatre. In Europe, Jan Kott's book has had an enormous influence, but in this country we have been dilatory in following the exciting paths that he has opened up. This is, I believe, because we still adhere to the last tatty remnants of a somewhat tacky classical heritage, and believe that Shakespeare must be performed as *he* intended. I have said that I do not know what he intended, because I have only myself to trust when I read his plays. All interpretation is subjective. A few years ago, *Hamlet* was the perfect Watergate play. Everybody was putting a bug under the table, or a tail on their son, and this was an area of *Hamlet* that could easily be examined and developed within the larger framework.

Then, three or four years ago, suddenly one of the great soliloquies in *Hamlet* sprang to life, 'How all occasions do inform against me', as twenty thousand people piled into aircraft carriers and ships, and set sail twelve thousand miles to fight for a little plot of ground that wasn't big enough to bury the numbers of people who were going to be killed on it. It may only be one aspect of the play, but one would be failing in one's duty as a director, if at the time of the Falklands War, one had not made the audience absolutely aware of what was being said in that speech, and its complete relevance to today. The government was sending the same number of men, twenty thousand, to fight for a barren piece of ground so poor that, for five ducats, I would not farm it.

Those are the things that make plays go in and out of

focus. Suddenly, contemporary events relate absolutely to the matters with which the play is concerned. One can start with the pre-history of *Hamlet*, and go back thirty years before the start of the play to the battle fought between Old Hamlet and Old Fortinbras, the day that Hamlet was born, a date pinpointed absolutely and precisely by the grave-diggers. And what has happened in those thirty years? Denmark has been running down, all those old battles, those old warriors resting on their laurels. And suddenly the forces are massing on the borders of Denmark again, not a band of lawless resolutes, but a highly organized army. What does Claudius do? He sees that his country is falling apart and his brother is not doing anything about it. Why does he kill old Hamlet? It can't be just because he loves Gertrude. *Nobody* just takes over a country, killing the king or the president or the dictator and taking over every aspect of ruling, governing and controlling, just for love.

And what then does Claudius do? He institutes a twenty-four-hour, seven-days-a-week, arms race. You can see the Exocets, the MIGs piling up! Twenty-four hours a day, the blast furnaces keep going. Why? Because the country has to be set on a war footing. Any production of *Hamlet* that does not create that atmosphere, and understand the reasons behind it, does not reflect the play that Shakespeare has written.

Unfortunately in Britain, we have been influenced by some wonderfully jingoistic productions of *Henry V*, *Richard III* and *Hamlet* by Sir Laurence Olivier, which managed to cut out some of the most essential ingredients of the plays themselves. His film version of *Henry V* cuts the play by some fifteen hundred lines, and so you lose all the disturbing elements, the things that make you wonder whether *Henry V* really is a hymn to the glory of England. The Olivier film of *Hamlet* cut out Fortinbras, cut out Rosencrantz and Guildenstern, and so emasculates Claudius. We inherit a distorted view of these plays, which have been handed down to us through great *tour de force* performances. To restore these plays to their original purposes, we have to analyse every single aspect of those rather awkward parts of the plays which cannot be ignored. It's often around the edges, on the fringes, that you find those small characters, the apparently minor ones, who throw a bomb into the pool and blow all the big fish out. An actor, a director, a group of people working on the text have to make sense of every single line. You can't brush one detail under the carpet, or cut it, because you don't understand it.

In *Romeo and Juliet*, for example, during the party scene with the Capulets, Romeo who is masked grabs a serving man and says, 'Who's that girl over there?' And the serving man takes a look and says, 'I know not, sir!' What is a serving man doing in that house and at that party if he doesn't know the daughter of the household? What are the choices? Outside catering? Is Juliet so heavily masked that he doesn't recognize her? In which case, why does Romeo say, 'Oh she doth teach the torches to burn bright'? Or is the servant just an idiot? Do you play him like a fool? Directors have to cope with problems like that, but finding the balance between that question, that serving man and Juliet is what constitutes the excitement. It is in such details that the bridge can be built between the stage and the market place.

But finally, whatever critics may say, whatever the playwright might ultimately have thought, all can change when the actor steps up to speak the lines, because the present, past and future of the theatre rests in the hands of the actors. Actors can change, if they so wish, the meaning of any play that has been written. A line on a page does not exist as a piece of theatre. A whole play does not exist when it's simply in print. It only exists when it is performed, and at that moment, and for that moment, only.

One night, somebody's broken a leg, someone is having a divorce, the company are in the middle of a row, the house is only half-full, and the whole audience has a cold, and it's terrible. The next night, somebody's won a hundred thousand pounds, the audience has come in coachloads, two people have got engaged, there's a champagne party, and the sun's shining, and it's the best performance in the world. One audience goes out, saying, 'Don't go to see that! It's awful!' and the other audience says, 'It's the best night I've had in years!'

Which is right? They're both right, because the actuality

of the performance *is* what is contemporary about it. When an actor steps up and changes 'To be or not to be' into 'To be or *not* to be?' or '*To* be or *not* to be!', then that is his interpretation, which is a response to the pressures of the moment. I can't say what the line *means*. I can only offer an idea of it in context, but the actor may change the whole interpretation according to his or her view of what has happened on the way to the theatre – or to what they may have read in the newspapers. That is the only way that the theatre can take place. That is the only way of performing Shakespeare. He must be, he is and always will be our contemporary.

At this point, several members of the audience wanted to challenge Bogdanov's sturdy defence of Kott, but Martin Esslin asked them to be patient until the other main contributors had spoken. He then turned to the artistic director of the Young Vic, David Thacker.

Thacker's production of Ibsen's *Ghosts* with Vanessa Redgrave, which had just opened at the Young Vic, much impressed the international critics and was on its way to a successful West End run. It confirmed his reputation as one of Britain's best young directors. Through his work at the Young Vic, he had managed to build up lively and committed student audiences for Shakespeare without being dismissed by older minds as too trendy. In the week of the seminar, he had started rehearsals for *Julius Caesar* and he began by describing how his actors had discussed the play's meaning and why they should be tackling the play at all. What were they trying to communicate? The social context for him was of the utmost importance and he illustrated what he meant by one vivid example.

DAVID THACKER: When I was a student, I directed *Pericles* which we took to the Edinburgh Festival, and as part of our warm-up for Edinburgh, we went to perform in a long-term prison. Many people there were in for life, including, sitting in the middle of the front row, Ian Brady, the Moors murderer. *Pericles*, as you know, deals with incest, rape and child-murder, and for the first twenty minutes, you knew quite well on whose side the audience was. They applauded the notion of violent attacks on young girls, because they weren't accustomed to this theme being handled in the theatre at all. Most of them had probably never been to a theatre; and it's obviously quite exciting, if you're in a long-term prison, to have three or four attractive young students coming in to perform a play like *Pericles*.

But when we had got half-an-hour into the play, it started to impose its hold on the audience. By the time that we had reached the reconciliation scene where Pericles meets his daughter unknown to him, although her identity becomes clear in the course of the scene, men were weeping buckets. At the end, the applause was tumultuous. I have never experienced a comparable reaction. I knew then instantly what was the point of doing Shakespeare. It is to touch chords in the hearts of the audience, so that they can place their own experiences in the context of a work that a great artist has provided for them, and can recognize that their experiences are not entirely personal to themselves but are shared by a broad cross-section of humanity.

Jan Kott has already mentioned Hamlet's remarks about the actors as 'the abstract and brief chronicles of the time'. Hamlet also said that their purpose was to hold the mirror up to nature, 'to show virtue her own feature, scorn her own image, and the very age and body of the time his form and pressure'. I understand 'abstract and brief chronicles' to mean something like newspapers, and that the actors are there to show people what the times they are living in are really like. That's why Hamlet valued acting so highly, and that is Shakespeare's way of describing the purpose of doing a play at all, to show people their own contemporary world.

The problem nowadays as a director is that there has been a chronic over-exposure to Shakespeare's plays. You don't often find in the theatre that pure relationship which we discovered with *Pericles* in that long-term prison, where the inmates had never heard of the Prince of Tyre and who Shakespeare was anyway. They just came to see a play which might or might not affect them. Normally, however, when you are directing Shakespeare, you feel as a director the pressure of having to prove something. How will this production be seen in some kind of historical development? Will it be a major re-evaluation of the play? What will the critics think?

The only way to protect yourself as a practitioner against that kind of pressure is to look to your audiences and to think about why you're doing the play at all. The great privilege of directing Shakespeare at the Young Vic is that a very large proportion of the audiences will never have seen the play and do not have any kind of vested interest in seeing it performed like this or like that. They just want to be grabbed by the play so that they understand it, probably for the first time.

And so we approach our productions like this. We in a sense try to imagine that Shakespeare is working alongside us and that we are doing it for people who have never seen the play before. We are not doing it for people who have seen it a hundred times before. If the play emerges as a fresh, new and vigorous re-evaluation of the text, that's accidental too. It just happens in the process. The aim is to find what the play is about and how to make that meaning clear.

If you're doing a new play, your aim is to express that play as fully as you can, so that the production and the play are united. You may never achieve that union, but that is your goal. The difficulty with Shakespeare after four hundred years is that you cannot achieve that sort of perfect consummation, because sometimes the words cannot have a literal and accurate representation within the play. In *Julius Caesar*, for example, you have to decide whether you are going to do it in Elizabethan costume, doublet-and-hose or whatever, because otherwise many words will not ring absolutely, centrally, true. If Cassius talks about his doublet 'unbrac'd' to the storm, you know that Shakespeare was not imagining that he was really wearing a toga; but to do the production in doublet-and-hose is bound to be confusing and alienating for an audience. You have to try to find some metaphorical equivalent, so that you can bring out the play's central direction, its most crucial issues and ideas. What is frustrating, however, is that you know that you can never really succeed, because there will be internal contradictions which will inevitably scupper all your efforts. That is the difference between working on a four-hundred-year-old text and a modern one.

We should really think in terms of three historical moments. The first is the time about which Shakespeare was writing, the second is the time when he was writing and the third is the time when we receive the play in performance. In *Julius Caesar*, there is a thrust of sympathy in the early part of the play towards those who want to get rid of this dictatorial leader. Whatever the weaknesses or inadequacies of the conspirators, what is clear when you work on the text is this drive to get rid of that person. You then have to ask questions about Shakespeare's motives. Was he behind or not this move to oust the dictator? Did he approve of it? What was he saying to his own age, when he writes about the Romans?

Then you have to ask whether this Roman world was different from his own, and in what respect. The more I direct Shakespeare, the more inclined I am to think that it is always his own world about which he is writing, even in plays that are full of images of the pagan world and ancient customs. In *King Lear*, for example, we would typically imagine clubs and furs and ancient Britons, whereas in fact the language is chock-full of Jacobean references.

Gloucester says to Edmund when he finds him with the letter, 'What paper were you reading?', and Edmund answers, 'Nothing, my lord!'. Gloucester replies, 'If it be nothing, I shall not need spectacles.' Can you imagine a man with a club and furs walking around with spectacles? Gloucester says, 'Who brought it?' and Edmund replies, 'I found it thrown in at the casement of my closet.' There aren't many closet casements in Druid ruins.

Shakespeare always seems to imagine that the play is happening now. He always treats his subject in some kind of contemporary idiom. It seems to have been a theatrical convention of his time. For us, that is impossible. It isn't possible simply to do *King Lear* in modern dress, because we find the same problem in a different disguise. You don't have casement windows in your modern, high-tech pad. The only alternative is to take a leap of courage. You have to attempt to understand what the drift of the play was for Shakespeare and then search for some close contemporary equivalent that will make the play precise, clear and immediate for the audience. I try to do this through stage images which clarify the function of a character or a particular moment in the play.

24

Let me give an example. In our production of *Hamlet*, we dressed Polonius as an executive politician in a civil service suit, so that audiences could immediately recognize the kind of man he was, his role in the state. When he says goodbye to Laertes, he writes him a cheque, so that it is clear that Laertes has plenty of money, which comes from his father. A simple image like that can make a passage immediately clear to an audience, and that is what we are always trying to do, to communicate to *our* audiences in *our* time today. If we play Shakespeare at all, we have got in this sense to make him our contemporary.

Here Martin Esslin intervened. He agreed that from the point of view of working directors, Shakespeare's plays had to be produced in such a way that their interest is brought out for contemporary audiences; but 'from a slightly more detached point of view', he argued, 'there are various approaches both to making Shakespeare our contemporary and treating him as someone who wrote at a particular moment in history'.

MARTIN ESSLIN: Brecht's concern, for example, was *not* to convince his audiences that the conditions shown in *Pericles* or *Hamlet* are the same as today's, or indeed that human nature is a constant. Brecht wanted to place the situation *within* history, to show, for example, that Othello is not embodying the unchanging nature of male jealousy when he strangles Desdemona, but that he represents the seventeenth-century idea that women are the properties of their husbands. You get very angry if somebody else is stealing or using your property. Therefore there is a school of thought which argues that you should present Shakespeare as an object lesson in historical materialism and historical change.

But of course, Shakespeare's plays do embody human emotions that haven't changed, or only very little. Think of *King Lear* and all those plays and novels written today about children trying to get rid of their fathers by putting them into old age homes. The tension between these two approaches is one of the most interesting features of current Shakespearian productions.

Brecht also said that classics only have the value of raw material. They have no value *except* as raw material. This is where there is so much controversy between the purists and the modernists who take a Shakespeare play and re-write it. Sometimes Shakespeare in translation has this advantage, that a word like 'doublet' does not have to be in another language so historically explicit. But we will discuss that question in another session. Brecht, of course, went much further. In his adaptation of *Coriolanus*, he cut and changed a number of lines in such a way that he turned the accepted meaning of the play on its head. The tribunes became the heroes, not the villains.

That is one of the strengths of Shakespeare. His plays provide a kind of multi-focal viewpoint. You can look at the play as it was written. You can treat it as a historical document. You can consider what it means to you as an expression of continuing human emotions and you can look at it again as a myth which lives through its ability to be modified. You can take *Coriolanus* and change the scene with Volumnia around, so that Coriolanus does not attack Rome because he loves his mother and his wife and his children, but because he has become convinced that they have a better armaments factory than they had before and that he hasn't got a chance of winning. By doing that, you not only have a different play, but you are also commenting on the old one for audiences who, unlike those in David Thacker's long-term prison, know the original very well, and will grasp the point of turning it around.

And then there is the question of the re-writing of Shakespearian themes by modern authors. *Endgame*, as Jan Kott has pointed out, is a paraphrastic treatment of *The Tempest*, as is Edward Bond's *The Sea*. Indeed Bond has used this technique very often, in his *Lear*, his *The Sea*; and in *Bingo*, he presents Shakespeare himself on stage as a character. We use Shakespeare's plays in exactly the same way as the Greeks developed their compendium of myths, through Homer, Hesiod or whichever versions were familiar at that time; and indeed as Shakespeare used the myths of *his* time. That is perhaps what makes Shakespeare our contemporary. His stories have helped to make up the fabric of our civilization, certainly in Britain but, I think, all over Europe.

One European country more reluctant than others to accept Shakespeare's plays within 'its cultural fabric' was France. Before Victor Hugo championed Shakespeare, Voltaire had denounced him as a barbarian and for some French critics, though not Guy Dumur, this argument is by no means settled.

Dumur is the critic for the Paris paper *Le Nouvel Observateur*, who spoke in French and through an interpreter. He began by pointing out that it had only been in the past thirty or forty years that Shakespeare's plays had been produced widely and regularly in France. In that sense, he had only recently become their contemporary.

Many plays were not performed in France until recently, particularly the histories, including *Richard II*, *King John* and the two parts of *Henry IV*. French directors do not have the established tradition within which Shakespeare can be produced. They had to make that tradition. This is why French directors have been more experimental in their approach. Dumur took issue with Kott over Ariane Mnouchkine's Shakespearian productions. She did not direct in a specifically Japanese style, but in an oriental one, using many kinds of traditions from Indian, Balinese, Persian, Chinese, and Japanese theatres. There was no attempt to produce a Kabuki Shakespeare.

Shakespeare, Dumur argued, was a man of his time. He was an Elizabethan in all of his plays, which didn't prevent him from providing a telling commentary from that perspective on events which are close to us today, for example, on how Hitler or Stalin behaved. The problem for a director is how to make that Elizabethan perspective clear in its contemporary context; and sometimes a director may be tempted to sacrifice what is Elizabethan in Shakespeare in order to reinforce the modern significance. In one recent French production of *Richard III* by Georges Lavandant, the characters were handled as caricatures, with the tragedy of the situation emerging as subsidiary to the comedy. In Roger Planchon's version of *Henry IV* in 1958, Prince Hal was treated as a thug throughout. He never behaved like a prince and the future Henry V. He even stabs Hotspur in the back. 'That may be a distortion, but it is one which comes from one of the determinations of French directors to get away from the nineteenth-century, Romantic Shakespeare.'

'That begs the question', said Martin Esslin, 'as to whose interpretation is right or wrong. You have used the word distortion to apply to Planchon's interpretation of the text, but it is one which can be supported by textual evidence. Distortion is in the eye of the beholder, somebody who knows the play beforehand and has interpreted it in a different way.'

There were several cries of 'No' from the audience, which drove Esslin on to develop this point in more detail.

MARTIN ESSLIN: There is certainly a case for presenting Hal as a thug. In Part Two, he is still lounging around taverns.

Historically, he punched the Lord Chief Justice, got arrested and thrown in the Fleet, jailed! And so Planchon wasn't necessarily distorting Shakespeare when he showed Hal as a thug. Our inherited view as to what Shakespeare meant has distorted Hal by turning him into a hero prince.

Traditional ideas may also be distortions. The inherited view of Hamlet is that he is a thin, pale man, whereas the part was written for Richard Burbage at the age of thirty-seven, when he weighed seventeen and a half stone. 'Fat and scant of breath' was probably nearer the mark. The textual evidence from the grave-diggers' scene indicates that Hamlet was thirty and in Elizabethan society, girls were married when they were twelve. And so you have a thirty-year-old son of a king, messing about with a twelve-year-old girl. That was the social situation, but our inherited view of Hamlet is very different. Distortions come with prior knowledge, which is why, as David Thacker has said, it can be very refreshing to hear the reactions of schoolchildren who have not seen the play before and make up their minds without prejudice.

That, agreed Dumur, was also one of the advantages of being a French director. Because they were not working within an established tradition and lacked the power of the poetry in English, they could look at the plays with innocent eyes and try different ways technically to make them work. But he accepted Esslin's distinction between interpretation and distortion.

At this point, Erich Fried entered the theatre, walking slowly to the platform with the aid of a stick.

No living English poet, and very few elsewhere in the world, could claim the kind of following that Fried can command among German-speaking countries, where his books are sold in print-runs of a hundred thousand copies and his poetry readings fill theatres larger than the Albert Hall.

He was brought up in Vienna and his family, who were Jewish, suffered under Nazism. Fried fled to London and eventually joined the German language section of the BBC. He has translated Dylan Thomas, T.S. Eliot and Shakespeare.

An admirer of Marx who points out that 'Marx insists that we must question everything', including communism, a member of the influential German writers' association, Gruppe 47, Fried is celebrated for his witty, often polemical and brilliantly inventive verses and stories, the left-wing conscience (as he was once described) of the German-speaking peoples.

His recent serious illnesses had not impaired the rich quality of his voice or the expressivity of his features which had made him so effective a performer. After Esslin had introduced him to the audience and he had apologized for being late, Fried immediately returned to the central question, 'Is Shakespeare still our contemporary?'

ERICH FRIED: Obviously it all depends on what we understand by 'contemporary'. If we mean 'stop-press-news', then Shakespeare is not a contemporary, or only accidentally, and his plays can be misused if they accidentally strike upon some very ephemeral topic of the moment. But there is another approach.

It is often said that yesterday's writers seem to be more out of date than those of two or three generations before. That is because we are disappointed by the fact that they are not absolutely contemporary in the narrowest sense of the word. We don't realize that we are called upon to make the effort to see the more lasting patterns of behaviour, from which emerges a deeper understanding of what is happening to people today and what has happened in past civilizations.

I do not mean 'timeless'. Nothing is timeless. If we read ancient Assyrian stories, we find that we cannot easily identify with them, because the distance between their experiences and ours is too great. Even if we try to understand the meaning of honour in Homer, we find that the code of the Greek heroes is more closely connected to the Samurai traditions than to ours. But if we look at the behaviour patterns in Shakespeare, and his profound understanding of the psychology of his characters, we find time and time again that Shakespeare's plays are not more outdated, and sometimes less, than, say Shaw's *Pygmalion* or Brecht's *Arturo Ui*.

I like *Arturo Ui* very much, but what happens in it is fifty years old, and Hitler is gone, and Hitler's rise to power is not our contemporary problem. Nevertheless, some of the behaviour patterns are still with us, such as how a dictator has originally been the tool of somebody else and changes when he comes to power, how he has to learn from an actor to perform, all those insights which still make sense to us, particularly with an actor in the White House! Similarly, in *Pygmalion*, the entire milieu may be outdated, but still today people are branded by the way they speak and are looked down upon because of their habits, and the person who tries to raise them has profoundly misunderstood the nature of the problem and is being, in fact, very condescending. These patterns persist, which is why Brecht and Shakespeare are still worth playing. But when we look at Shakespeare . . .!

When I was a child, I learnt Shakespeare in German, and Germans, being German, thought that Shakespeare was much better in German than in English, which only Germans could believe. We had all kinds of theories as to whether Polonius was really very wise or a fool. The English don't have those difficulties. They know that essentially Polonius was a fool. But the more serious problem was whether Hamlet was actually deranged or not. Here Shakespeare is so modern that only anti-psychiatry and the musings of a French Germanist [Pierre Bertaux], on Hölderlin, reach towards the same degree of actuality that Shakespeare had in his psychology. He shows in such a masterly way that lunacy makes sense. The nonsense of Ophelia's symptoms isn't nonsensical at all. The state of mind is something which was hardly shown again before psychoanalysis discovered these things.

Or look at a character like Falstaff, not in *The Merry Wives of Windsor*, which was more or less written to order, but in *Henry IV*. Falstaff is a raucously funny character, but at the same time, tremendously sad, a man who is more intelligent really, and more educated as far as we can tell from the remnants of his knowledge than any other person in the play, but who has lost his function and come down in the world. For me, he has parallels with Lucky in *Waiting for Godot* – and when you see how the playboy who is trying to do good, Henry, how he behaves towards Falstaff, most atrociously, you realize that Hal's turning good is not altogether turning towards Good.

Shakespeare had to provide a positive moral to the audience, but I believe that he was perfectly aware that there was another side to the question. He showed that double-sidedness to Henry's character, just as when later on in *Henry V*, Henry stands outside the gates of Calais and describes the horror of war, he who is about to inflict the horrors of war! The dialectics of the character have never been better demonstrated, not by any contemporary, although sometimes contemporary writers seem better, because they are more topical. One doesn't have to stress the importance of an anti-war play like *Troilus and Cressida*, but only perhaps to show how, for example, Shakespeare presents the character of Agamemnon, the man who holds office and has power, but where there is very little left of substance behind that power.

Or you have the opposite in *The Merchant of Venice*, where Shakespeare has provided his audience with a Jewish stock character, the evil usurer. A Jewish doctor had just been executed in London, on a false charge incidentally, and what does Shakespeare really do? Shylock is the only character in the play that has real depth, except perhaps, in much more fleeting brush strokes, Antonio, who is obviously homo-erotic and whose feelings Shakespeare sketches in a way far above what was done in the theatre at that time, far more psychologically knowledgeable. Wherever we look in his plays, we see how perceptive he is, when he really means to look at things seriously. Sometimes, even in England, we do not realize how hard-hitting he is.

I was reminded of this force when I had to translate *Hamlet*. When Hamlet says about the marriage of his mother following so soon after the funeral of his father, 'Thrift, thrift, Horatio, the funeral baked meats did coldly furnish forth the marriage tables', I translated this so that the allusion should be made clear that Hamlet is suggesting that his father's flesh was eaten at his mother's wedding. A German Shakespeare specialist objected that this allusion was not in Shakespeare, but he had forgotten that a baked meat casserole was at that time called a coffin.

This is mentioned in Shakespeare's time in several plays, including *Titus Andronicus*, when Titus kills the sons of Tamara and makes a pie out of them, and uses these very words as he describes in the last seconds of their life what will happen to them. This is the Shakespeare whom we wrongly in Germany try to describe as a baroque author. Of course, the various phases of the culture in one country cannot be exactly equated with the culture of another, but just as in Germany, only now are the baroque poets starting to be really understood, so we are now beginning to recognize how the deeper patterns in Shakespeare are still extremely meaningful, and that is essentially why he has been understood over the centuries.

He may not be our contemporary in the sense of being topical, but he is contemporary to our deeper behaviour patterns, and therefore he is very often able to show how society moves, how allies are betrayed out of fear and out of weakness, how (for example) Hotspur is let down by his father-in-law, how the conspiracy against Caesar works partly through slander and partly through correct statements. I could give many more examples.

Of course, Shakespeare may not be equally contemporary in all of his plays. When he caricatures fashions of his time, like the Academy in *Love's Labour's Lost*, all that is far removed from us. There are other examples in other plays, more in the comedies, I would say, than in the tragedies. But what about *Measure for Measure*? That's certainly a contemporary play, although whether it counts as a comedy must remain an open question.

Members of the audience were impatient to intervene. One suggested that the attempt to prove that Shakespeare is our contemporary was nothing more than the sustaining of the old myth that Shakespeare somehow managed to embody 'in some kind of permanent form, unchanging truths about human nature, which can then be applied to any time in any place. Aren't we by the very act of talking like this sustaining a mythology about human nature which ought to be subverted and de-mythologized?'

Martin Esslin agreed that every myth needed to be questioned, but added that if a society has not got a common body of referential material, it cannot engage in 'the dialectical process'.

MARTIN ESSLIN: That is the value of established canons of literary work to society. If you had a society with no such canons at all, a *tabula rasa*, there is no reference material. If I say that my relationship with my mother is different from that of Hamlet to his mother, it only makes sense if you know what Hamlet's relationship to his mother was like.

If you look at all the great revolutionary epochs, when society was really overthrown, the revolutionaries didn't start with a *tabula rasa*. Take the French Revolution. It was conducted from their literature in Roman terms. They recreated Brutus and Caesar. And look at the Russian Revolution. They made classical ballet the main point of reference in their artistic life, with Shakespeare and classical literature, and *insisted* that this was more important than starting from scratch, with a completely new literature.

If you take as a Marxist a dialectical view of history, then you can't get away from the pattern of one period reacting to another, and the material that one period has left behind becomes the basis on which you base your contradiction of that previous period. That is how Greek mythology became re-vitalized. That is how all mythology either dies or becomes re-vitalized.

DAVID THACKER: It's important to clarify that when you put a Shakespeare play in modern costume, you are not necessarily specifying that it is taking place in England now. What you are trying to do is to find a coherent metaphorical life within that production, so that the substance of the play, what is communicable and has contemporary connections, is brought home to the audience. You are not necessarily trying to confine it within any particular epoch.

Another member of the audience argued that the opposition between the 'classical approach' and the 'so-called contemporary one' was a false antithesis. Both views represented ideological positions, indeed political groupings. One was reactionary, the other revolutionary. 'We have been talking about the opposition between two political views, the old order and the new order. That is also what makes Shakespeare so exciting, the fact that he reflects a struggle between old and new, which was going on in his day as it is certainly going on in ours. He was writing about the new order, which was Protestant and bourgeois, and the old, which in his case meant feudal and aristocratic.'

It was, however, nearly lunchtime.

'I am sure', said Martin Esslin, tidying up his papers, 'that we will have a chance to discuss that question in later sessions.'

*

Thus, the platform speakers in the first session agreed that, in one sense or another, Shakespeare could and should be treated as our contemporary. There were, however, hints that there was another side to the story, from the audience, from Esslin who described the 'dialectical process' whereby a society uses old stories as 'referential material' and from Kott himself, who suggested that Shakespeare was now less of a contemporary because we were living in a 'Wittenberg', not an 'Elsinore'.

But the Kott approach, even as modified, begs many questions, some of which were to be addressed in later discussions. Some of the critics, however, spent lunch in considering our use of the word 'contemporary', as if it were a kind of compliment. It seems to make Shakespeare a more 'relevant' and 'accessible' writer. Shakespeare himself would not have shared that view. He would not have thought that Plautus was a more interesting writer because, with a stretch of the imagination, he might have shopped in Southwark. Shakespeare, in short, did not believe in evolution, unlike modern Europeans, even at their most self-critical. Did this difference of outlook separate us, not just from Shakespeare, but from many contemporary Eastern cultures, which don't believe in evolution either?

DOES SHAKESPEARE TRANSLATE?

with
**Alexander Anikst, Jean-Michel Déprats,
Erich Fried and, in the chair,
Carlos Tindemans**

Contemporary British audiences find Shakespeare's language difficult enough. He uses many unfamiliar words, but that is simply where the problems start, for he also employs Elizabethan rhetorical devices with great skill. Our ears are not trained to catch the tricks of assonance, dissonance, changing stresses within the verse line, alliteration and punning rhymes.

We also value words differently. We are more careful about spelling and precise definitions. The rationalization of the English language was one of our eighteenth-century legacies, particularly from the publication in 1755 of Dr Johnson's *Dictionary*. From then on, there was an authority to which we could refer, if we wanted to know whether we were using words correctly; and a correct use of language was something which distinguished the educated middle classes from the poor or the modish.

Shakespeare, however, delighted in the many different meanings which could be compacted into a word or a phrase, one reason why he uses so many puns. He relied upon his ear and common usage and the associative logic of a language which had not yet been disciplined by Neo-Classical rules. He even invents words.

This is roughly the difference between a denotative and a connotative use of language. It provides one of the hidden barriers to understanding, because a modern audience may pick up one of the meanings to a Shakespearian line, not realizing that there may be others. If native English speakers have such problems with Shakespeare's language, then aren't non-English ones facing almost insurmountable hurdles? And yet throughout Europe there are translations of Shakespeare which claim to be as good as the original.

In this discussion, which took place in the Young Vic's studio theatre, we wanted to consider whether it was possible adequately to translate

35

Shakespeare. In the chair was Carlos Tindemans, Professor of Theatre Semiotics in the University of Antwerp. He began by asking Erich Fried how he had approached the problems of translating Shakespeare into German and what he had learnt about Shakespeare's plays as a result.

ERICH FRIED: I started by translating the poems of Dylan Thomas, the plays and poems of T.S. Eliot, and others – Synge's *The Tinker's Wedding*, for example. It was not at my own initiative that I started to translate Shakespeare. Some theatres asked me to make a new translation, and indeed I have never translated a Shakespeare play for which some theatre or television station did not ask, because I find it very useful in rehearsal to see whether my translations are as good as I fondly believe – or whether some things which I thought would come across perfectly well, fail to do so.

I said this morning that the Germans believed that Shakespeare was really better in their Schlegel/Tieck translations than in English; and I have since been told that this is not uniquely to their discredit, because others, the Hungarians for example, evidently believe the same. This shows that Shakespeare comes across to our audiences, despite our translations – or perhaps we should congratulate ourselves, because we all know that a really perfect translation is impossible. Even if you translate the sentence and the metre exactly, you can't usually have the same music of the vowels, or only very rarely, and if you try to translate all the puns in Shakespeare . . . well, it's impossible.

Most translators are helped by the fact that they only recognize a fraction of the puns; but if you realize that they exist and try to translate them, you soon learn that it just isn't possible. You either have to stick to the philological translation, and leave out some of the puns, or you decide not to impoverish the text and put in another pun near the one which you couldn't translate, persuading yourself that this is the way in which Shakespeare might have punned under the circumstances. This may be a very dubious practice, but it is sometimes better than impoverishing the text where punning seems necessary. And whether puns are necessary or not, can only be judged from Shakespeare himself.

All the attempts to improve upon Shakespeare in German are, I think, ludicrous. When Mercutio dies in *Romeo and Juliet*, he says 'A plague on both your houses!' three times. Schlegel had been taught at school, just as I was, that repetition is not elegant, and so he improved on it by giving Mercutio a different phrase each time, and also the word 'plague' was not quite respectable enough in those days and so the plague didn't happen. He wrote, 'To the devil with both your houses!' and 'Let the hangman get them . . .' and the third time, something else, but the plague didn't occur – which isn't so good, because the three-times repeated curse of a dying man has something magical in it, at least for the comparatively young Shakespeare. And also that curse is fulfilled. There is an outbreak of plague. The priest gets walled up in a house and cannot deliver the letter to Mantua, and so the two people die. In the Schlegel translation, this connection is lost, because 'the plague' hasn't been translated.

And so when Shakespeare uses the same form of words several times, I try to use the same form in translation. I don't think that one should try to improve upon it.

Another reason why Schlegel was held to be better than Shakespeare is because he is sometimes more beautiful than the original. This is undeniable. For example, when in the fifth act of *A Midsummer Night's Dream*, Shakespeare writes, 'And this ditty after me, Sing and dance it trippingly', the German translation has 'Singt nach meiner Lieder Weise! Singet! hupfet! lose! leise!', which is much more poetic, and incidentally not a translation at all. But unfortunately, Shakespeare uses this couplet just as an introduction to Oberon's blessing of the elves and reserves the beauty of expression for the actual blessing, the highlight as it were, whereas Schlegel translated the introduction in this case more beautifully than the blessing itself. And Shakespeare would have laughed about that, because it is contrary to the dramatic effect.

Nevertheless in order to see how good even a bad Schlegel translation can be, one only has to compare it with Goethe's miserable adaptation of Schlegel's *Romeo and Juliet*, where he goes out of his way to ennoble it. For example, the Nurse speaks rather deftly and enjoys the idea that Juliet will have to have sex when she gets married, and Goethe puts all that into verse and raises it to an Iphigenian level, and all the puns and bawdy undercurrents of the play are left out and the result is supremely boring.

In German, the Schlegel translations – sometimes called the Schlegel/Tieck translations, because August Wilhelm von Schlegel only translated eighteen plays and the rest were done by Tieck with other members of the Schlegel family – were held to be masterpieces. I doubt whether this is really so. They have worked very well and found some wonderful solutions. I have been blamed in my translations – and I have translated twenty-six Shakespeare plays – for not throwing Schlegel aside altogether and taking no notice of him. I think that that would be wrong, not only because he found some very good solutions, but also because the understanding of Shakespeare in Germany has largely been formed by these Schlegel translations. To disregard them altogether, particularly where he hasn't misunderstood Shakespeare, would be presumptuous. Where he has misunderstood Shakespeare, of course, his version cannot be upheld.

He often falsified. For example, Romeo's and Juliet's parents, who are wealthy citizens, are raised by Schlegel to the level of high nobility. This makes nonsense of Juliet's father's pride at having found her a real nobleman for her husband. In fact, the entire background society is spoiled by not recognizing that the only noblemen around are the Duke, Mercutio and Paris – nobody else in the play. If that had not been so, the Duke could not so easily have banished Romeo.

Such mistakes, of course, can be easily rectified. What is also said in the defence of Schlegel is that he didn't have such good Shakespearian texts as we have, nor such good English dictionaries. All this is true, although, as a matter of fact, Schlegel's knowledge of English was magnificent. His power of language in German is not always so good. To transfer Shakespeare's blank verse into Schlegel's, he very often uses the present participle and devices like that, which make his translations look sometimes like that of a student.

The English use the present participle more familiarly than the Germans do; and it can be dubious to use the same construction.

Sometimes Schlegel uses complicated constructions in order to versify what in Shakespeare are simple, straightforward constructions. Shakespeare reserves his complicated constructions for state speeches – or for Malvolio, when he tries to be very important – but Schlegel sometimes makes things sound involved where they should be simple.

There were other German translations before Schlegel's, for example, those of Friedland, which were rather slovenly, but with greater power of language than Schlegel in many cases could command; and Schlegel, despite criticizing him strongly, plundered his translations to no mean extent. Then there were other German translations after Schlegel, which were very good, but suffered from the fact that they were written at the beginning of the Wilhelminian era, when German had become rather debased as a language by the misuse of words. And so the words are for us suspect whereas they were all right at the time. I am thinking of Gildemeister. And later on, Gundolf looked through and corrected the Schlegel translations with great love, but where Schlegel had left out puns that he considered too frivolous, Gundolf puts them back again, but very heavily and certainly not frivolously. That wasn't such a happy solution.

One of the most interesting attempts to translate Shakespeare was made in the eighteenth century by Eschenburg, a Professor of English, and very good, a man who knew Shakespeare very well. He did prose translations, because he tried to get near the original and the poetic undertones. Of course, one can't really make prose translations of Shakespeare in the long run, because it is not for nothing that he didn't write prose throughout, but wrote partly in prose and partly in verse. Sometimes, the difference between them is due to various versions and is not absolutely convincing, as in *The Two Gentlemen of Verona*, but in his more mature and better plays, one can always see why there is verse somewhere and prose somewhere else.

But for translators today, the Eschenburg version is invaluable, because it translates Shakespeare into a German that is still completely understandable to us but still is a German before the Industrial Revolution came to Germany, and so jarring new words have not been used. One can keep the imaginative distance, where such a distance should be kept and which is lost when the words are too up-to-date.

Another translator whom I normally admire very much, Michael Hamburger, uses a modern German expression in his translation of *The Tempest*, 'mit Akribie', which means 'in very great detail', but it's a completely modern phrase. It jars terribly; and there is no artistic reason to use it. We all make such mistakes but they shouldn't happen.

Nowadays, German universities are producing interlinear versions, that is, *verbatim* German translations of the Shakespeare text, compiled by experts. These versions compared with the Eschenburg are completely useless for the translator. They may have some value for those who do not know enough English in the first place, but they shouldn't be translating Shakespeare anyway. The undertones and overtones of the text are entirely lost, which is exactly what Eschenburg tried to avoid by not sticking to the verse. These interlinear versions are incredibly dull.

I don't want to speak very much about my own translations, but it's not easy to avoid because I have translated so many Shakespeare plays. Of course, I have tried to preserve both the content and, as far as possible, the artistic form that Shakespeare uses. This is not always possible. In *Hamlet*, to take a famous example, where Hamlet says to Ophelia, 'Get thee to a nunnery!', we know that a nunnery is a holy house of nuns and, at the same time, an expression for a brothel. That double meaning does not exist in German and so it cannot be translated. I interpolated there, 'Go to the good virgins', to the 'guten Jungfrauen', because the 'guten Jungfrauen' were always known to be prostitutes in Germany. And so you have something like the 'nunnery' image realized by the insertion of three or four more words than the author used, which is a dubious practice, but acceptable perhaps in this case to save the double meaning that Schlegel lost entirely – 'Geh in ein Kloster, Ophelia'. I did similar translations of Dylan Thomas, with his approval, when he was alive.

Despite all that, I think it is possible to translate Shakespeare's plays. It is a wonderful advantage to be able to use old words. I never knowingly use words that cropped up in German after the Industrial Revolution, because I don't think that one should try forcibly to make Shakespeare contemporary. That can be done, but it is not a translation but an adaptation. It may have its special charms, but it is a different thing.

The impossibility of translating Shakespeare's text and doing justice to the original is shown most clearly not in the plays but in the sonnets, because German is a language full of prefixes and suffixes which English does mostly without. The sonnet lines either become so long that they don't work any more or else you have to leave out half the words. There have been many attempts to translate the sonnets, but none have really worked.

Lastly, I want to speak about translating Shakespeare into English. In German, I have the advantage of being able to use words that are no older than the end of the eighteenth century, words that are easy to understand but not painfully modern. In English, you are presented with texts that are much older, sixteenth- and seventeenth-century texts. Many words are difficult for the average English listener to understand; and there have been attempts to modernize Shakespeare. One play was translated by Robert Graves in such a way that he only used words which existed in Shakespeare's time, but words that could still be understood – and he left in very old-fashioned words only where Shakespeare wanted somebody, like Malvolio, to use old-fashioned or dusty speech.

I thought this was a remarkable attempt, but it was received with horrified dislike by the English theatre critics of the day. I remember one review by Milton Shulman that I thought was most unfair. I think that this is a worthwhile endeavour – not, for God's sake, to use *basic* English, which would impoverish Shakespeare as it has enfeebled the Bible – but one which makes a greater allowance in the use of language. Graves tried, as translators into other languages have tried, to use words that are not too modern but to select from the old words available those which are easily

41

understandable, as Shakespeare would have wanted them to be.

Tindemans asked whether these problems in Shakespearian translation were common to other European countries; and he turned to Alexander Anikst as a scholar rather than a translator for an answer.

Until his death in 1988, Anikst was the Chairman of the Soviet Shakespeare Commission. His father had been one of Lenin's closest associates. The family was in exile with Lenin in Zurich, before returning to Russia in 1917 to take part in the October Revolution.

Under Stalin, the whole family suffered. Anikst's father was shot arbitrarily and without trial, his mother sent to a concentration camp. Anikst himself was branded as a 'cosmopolitan', Stalinist newspeak for Jewish traitor, partly because he spoke English. He could only resume his studies after Stalin's death in 1953, by which time (he later told me) he wanted to concentrate on the 'great writers', by which he meant Shakespeare and the Greek classical dramatists.

ALEXANDER ANIKST: I come from the Soviet Union. So little is known about our literature, art and theatre, and so much is misconceived about our life, that I feel I should introduce myself a little bit immodestly. I represent here one of our biggest institutions of scholarship, the Institute of the History of the Arts, which studies and does research work into all fields of art. All arts and modern arts are what is now called communications and information. That is what I am paid for.

And I am also a Shakespeare scholar – and have written six books on Shakespeare, not all of them original, because it is important to give Soviet readers the gist, the synthesis of what is being done by modern Shakespearian scholarship in England, America, Germany and France. In this capacity, I was elected Chairman of the Soviet Shakespeare Commission, which is the kind of work that is unpaid, although there is a great deal of trouble attached to it.

As a representative of both the Institute and the Shakespeare Commission, I am connected with our theatres. Soviet theatres, when they stage Shakespeare, consult scholars – to tell them what's this and what's that, to explain Shakespeare. There is one question to which I haven't found an answer. They asked me at one theatre where they were staging *Othello*, 'What kind of military greeting was there in Venice or in England when Othello was Commander-in-Chief?' If anyone can inform me on that point, I shall be very grateful.

Russia is like Germany, a very Shakespeare-ized country. We also started our acquaintance with Shakespeare in the mid-eighteenth century, but under different political conditions. The first Russian translation of Shakespeare was of *Hamlet* by our classical writer, Sumarokov. But this was very awkward, because it was the time when Catherine the Great with her minions and guards had killed her husband, who made her Empress of Russia; and her son Paul was, of course, in disfavour. And so to translate *Hamlet* under those conditions was very risky. Therefore, the author had to make a lot of changes in the text to prevent them from taking the text too literally as an allusion.

The second important translation of Shakespeare into Russian was of *Julius Caesar* by the great Russian historian Karamzin, who was a very conservative man, and why he chose to translate *Julius Caesar*, which is full of conspiracies and uprisings, I still cannot understand. And so the first Russian versions of Shakespeare were very free – and there was not much left of the real Shakespeare. But in the Romantic period, as in other countries, Shakespeare became the idol of modern writers. They started to imitate him – as did the founder of modern Russian literature, Pushkin, who wrote the famous tragedy *Boris Godunov*, which is not exactly an imitation but written under Shakespeare's inspiration.

There were other attempts to imitate Shakespeare, but at the same time they started translating him. In the 1840s, there was a great Russian actor, Mochalov, who played Hamlet, and he was lucky enough to have the greatest Russian critic, Belinsky, as his admirer, who left us a complete description of his performances. We can reconstruct the way he played Hamlet better than we can remember some more modern interpretations.

But the translation was still rather free. They inserted into Shakespeare what wasn't in the text, and it was only in the second half of the nineteenth century that they started to keep more or less closely to the original. And they were greatly helped in this by the Schlegels. Some translators, I suspect, translated Shakespeare not from the original but from Schlegel's German translations. Anyway, many Russian versions are closer to the German than the British texts. There are several names which should be mentioned in this connection, Alexander Kroneburg, who gave us the best nineteenth-century *Hamlet*, and Alexander Sokalovsky, who translated Shakespeare's plays completely.

You should realize that the Russian language has much longer words than English. You must not take me literally if I say that English is a language of four-letter words, whereas Russian is an eight-to-ten-letter word language. When they tried to translate Shakespeare, they always had to add a number of lines to the text to express everything that there was in the original. And so the nineteenth-century translations were in length what we may call six-act plays, because there were so many additional verses. The nineteenth-century translations were very wordy.

Well, even now Shakespeare isn't staged in the complete text. They cut him at the National Theatre and at the Royal Shakespeare Company as well. But with these six-act Shakespeare tragedies, they had to cut him even more. In the twentieth century, a reaction set in against these translations. You will be amused to know that a member of the Romanov family was one of the first to do a more or less exact translation of *Hamlet*. Konstantin Romanov was a poet, who published his early translation with two texts, English and Russian opposite, so that you could compare. There was only one liberty he took. Sometimes instead of the pentameter, instead of five-foot iambics, he made six-foot lines, to keep the Shakespearian line more or less complete. That was another decent translation.

After the Revolution, a new movement began in Shakespearian translation. There was a slogan – 'equilinear' translations, line for line. But how can that be done when Russian words are longer than English ones? Nevertheless, they tried. The master of this art was Mikhail Lozinski. He made a translation of *Hamlet* that was absolutely equal, line for line. He was a master of the Russian language: he also translated Dante's *The Divine Comedy*. But he solved the problems like this. He used a number of obsolete words. This helped him to keep his translation as close as possible to the original, and it sounds very well, but just a bit too archaic. He translated other plays of Shakespeare, *Othello*, *Macbeth*, but his *Hamlet* is a classic. I doubt whether in any other language there is such a faithful rendering of Shakespeare. But actors complain that it is difficult to speak the verses written by Lozinski and so, although it used to say on the posters 'The translation of Lozinski', the actors took some passages from the old Kroneburg translation. But only a specialist would know that.

During the 1930s and 40s, this was the leading movement. We had a complete edition of Shakespeare in eight volumes, edited by the late Professor Smirnov from Leningrad. But when England was already in the Second World War, and Russia still was not, the great poet Boris Pasternak decided to start translating Shakespeare, and in 1940 he published his translation of *Hamlet*. It was for the Moscow Art Theatre. Stanislavski, the great leader of the Moscow Art Theatre, was dead, and the company was run by his friend and colleague, Vladimir Nemirovich-Danchenko, who took Pasternak's translation and analysed it from a theatrical point of view, showing where it was inadequate.

Pasternak was very easy-going. When an editor told him, 'This line doesn't sound right', Pasternak would instantly offer five variations. And so, he took back his *Hamlet* translation and worked on it. To cut a long story short, he made five versions of *Hamlet*, because this was his first Shakespeare translation and he had to find the way. Besides that, he translated *Romeo and Juliet*, *Othello*, *King Lear* and *Antony and Cleopatra*. And the more he worked, the better his translations became. *Antony and Cleopatra* is a marvel.

What was Pasternak's theory of translation? When he published his first translation of *Hamlet*, he said in the introduction, 'I ask the reader to regard this as an original piece of dramatic writing.' Rather a bold statement, isn't it? But Pasternak's idea was that one should not translate, but should re-create, Shakespeare, to write the play as if Shakespeare were a Russian poet living amongst us, which is very important. Pasternak's translations are in the modern language, a language which everybody could understand. He said that you should imagine that Shakespeare had been transplanted to Russia, so that his characters talked in the same way that they spoke to people at the Globe. It was the language of the Globe audience. He wanted Russian spectators to have a live Shakespeare, a modern Shakespeare, a contemporary one. That was his contribution to the idea of making Shakespeare our contemporary.

When Pasternak's translations were published, theatres gave up using other translations, and they staged his, because they were in the language used by everybody – of course, not literally so, but it was the live Russian of the day, not archaic, and very poetic, because he found the way of turning Shakespeare's images and metaphors into Russian.

The next generation of Russian translators all followed Pasternak's lead. Professor Smirnov and I edited a complete new Shakespeare, which included a number of modern translations, and I edited a volume of Shakespeare's tragedies, all in Pasternak's translations, which was a very enjoyable task. I had the chance to look through Pasternak's different versions of *Hamlet*, to see how a great poet works on translating Shakespeare, how he tries to make the meaning clearer and, as Erich Fried has done, to give the additional meanings, wherever possible.

There is another important matter: Shakespeare's poetry. For nineteenth-century Russian readers, Shakespeare the poet practically did not exist. There were two translations of Shakespeare's sonnets by Russian poets, but they were very clumsy. Nobody could have guessed that they were written by a great poet. Here again the lead for the new movement was given by Boris Pasternak. Pasternak translated only two sonnets of Shakespeare, but he found the way to do so. After him, another contemporary Soviet poet, Samuil Marshak, made a complete translation of the sonnets, and all of Russia fell in love with Shakespeare the poet. The Marshak translation of the sonnets is wonderful. It has been done in such a way that it has become a great work of Russian poetry.

I had the pleasure of knowing Marshak and I published an edition of these sonnets, with my notes; but in a way, I am rather unhappy that I added my name to this edition, because there is a kind of madness in our country now, to translate Shakespeare's sonnets. Every month, I receive a packet of new translations, except that they are often not very original, only attempts to re-arrange Marshak's translation. Only recently have we had several people who have translated some sonnets, more or less decently, more or less poetically.

I have only given a brief sketch of what has been done to translate Shakespeare in Russia. We are planning to start a new translation of at least half of Shakespeare's plays, leaving Pasternak intact, but hoping that there will be new versions of the better known plays in our theatres. In our country, the translators have their own social organization, a branch of the Union of Soviet Writers. They are connected with our Shakespeare Commission and with our theatres. This work is being done, as it were, socially, collectively, because Shakespeare is a playwright whom our theatres want to stage. They like to have living versions of his plays, while on the concert platform, we often have recitals of Shakespeare's sonnets, sometimes interspersed with life stories of Shakespeare, trying to connect the sonnets with a certain account, imaginative, of course, about how they came to be written.

Finally, I want to give you a few figures about the printing of Shakespeare's works. The last collected edition, which was made by subscription, amounted to two hundred thousand copies. Eight volumes each in two hundred thousand copies, each play with an essay and, of course, notes. I recently edited a volume of Shakespeare's tragedies in Pasternak's translation which had a printing of half a million copies. That gives you some idea of the vast audience that we have for Shakespeare translations.

The last platform speaker was the young French writer, Jean-Michel Déprats, whose sharp, meticulous and musical translations have contributed greatly to the current revival of interest in Shakespeare in France. He spoke at first from a written text but apologized for not immediately addressing the fundamental questions which had already been raised – of 'translation' versus 'adaptation', of archaic versus modern vocabularies and of translating Shakespeare as 'literature' or 'theatre'.

JEAN-MICHEL DÉPRATS: Does Shakespeare translate? Let's analyse some of the problems connected with this question, starting with the assumption that Shakespeare's poetry does not translate. How can the musical softness of a line such as 'How sweet the moonlight sleeps upon this bank' be translated into French – or into any other language – in which the 'sweet, sleep' assonance is lost and where the long-drawn-out sounds do not exist? Sounds do not translate, and thus translation comes up against the different phonetic structures of languages. But the gist of a poem is its harmony, its music. Rhythm, metrics, rhyme are the main springs and elements of this harmony. Leaving them out, leaving out any single one of them, results in flattening out the original text. Thus it would not seem that it is fully possible to translate Shakespeare.

André Gide, who translated *Hamlet* and *Antony and Cleopatra*, wrote that 'though there is no writer who deserves translation more than Shakespeare, he is without doubt the most difficult playwright to translate. In no other case, is translation more likely to disfigure the original text.' To be convinced, it is enough to examine the first line of *Twelfth Night*: 'If music be the food of love, play on' – nine words, among which only one has more than one syllable. It is impossible to express all this in French in an equally short way. The fundamental difficulty of translating Shakespeare into French lies first in this difference of proportions, of volume, between languages. French takes more space, it simply uses more words.

Now the goal of translation as far as poetry is concerned is not only to communicate a meaning. It is also to reproduce an object, its rhythm, form and volume. French translations of Shakespeare thus appear too slow, too laboured. In Shakespeare, the images overlap and cascade over one another. The translator would like to keep such density, but in his effort to preserve it, he is often led to expand into a whole sentence the metaphor which in the English text is contained in a single word. All the poetic movement in this verbal knot is in translation like a broken spring.

Translation becomes explanatory. Logic is respected, but the poetry no longer works. Modern French no longer has the wonderful plasticity which made possible Rabelais' and Montaigne's verbal inventions. French syntax and grammar are too stiff. André Gide again: 'The translator only achieves fidelity both to the genius of the French language and to the genius of Shakespearian poetry, thanks to continual petty stratagems and minor tricks.' How can we translate a line like 'My poor fool is hanged' in *King Lear*, when any translation by a term of pity and endearment misses the reference to the Fool? How can we translate an apparently simple line as 'A poor Egyptian yet' in *Antony and Cleopatra*, where the meaning of the word, 'yet', is 'however', 'still', 'so far', 'from now on', 'again', 'besides' etc.? How can we translate Macbeth's 'She should have died hereafter', where 'hereafter' doesn't mean 'later', but, according to Middleton Murry, 'in a different mode of time than that in which Macbeth is imprisoned now'?

When you have to translate, you either choose a precise meaning and lose the complexity of the line, and the ambiguity of the word, or you decide upon a more complex analytical rendering – and then use more words. Not to mention the problem of the puns, not an easy matter, as any translator knows. How do you translate into French, or into any other language, 'I live by the church', when 'by' means 'near' and 'through' the church?

But all this is what I would call the tedious litany of the cruxes of translation. It does not mean that Shakespeare does not translate at all. He does translate into French, probably better than Racine translates into English. There are lines in Racine of pure verbal magic, as there are in Shakespeare, of course; but in Racine, they are isolated gems of poetry, whereas in Shakespeare, we have to deal with gestic poetry, poetry in action, which has an undeniable concreteness. The sensory implication of the words uttered gives body in the literal meaning of that word to the elusive abruptness and wide sweep of Shakespeare's images.

Linguistically, the conflict is between the different ways of visualization between French and English. English, with its more concrete point of view, its more visualized attitude, seeks out detail in a way that the analytical French intellectual viewpoint refuses. But when the main endeavour in translation is to preserve the physicality, the concreteness and theatrical energy of the imagery, the translator has to struggle against the 'genius of his language'. He may be driven to translate for the benefit of the translated language, not for the benefit of the translating language. In order to let the new verbal forms required by the radical strangeness of Shakespeare's writing emerge, the translator has to resist the tyranny of those linguistic and mental patterns which are thought insepar-able from the genius of the French language, such as clarity, fluidity, logic, good taste, etc. If he doesn't struggle in this way, he is driven inevitably to make the text more explicit, or to tone it down, or to adorn it.

For me, the main requirement is to preserve the perform-ability of the text. Translating Shakespeare for the stage forces one to discover an oral and a gestic language, to give the actor precise material to work with. Thus, in a way, you translate *theatre* rather than simply *for* the theatre, a phrase which suggests that you are adapting something for an external goal. In that respect, literary translations, meant for the eye but not the ear, preclude an essential dimension of the text.

A play by Shakespeare, written by an actor for actors, is a theatre script in which the word order, the rhythms and images imply certain gestures, where the sensory character-istics of the words are to be an instrument for the player. Taking into account the dimension of the performance is not, in my view, damaging to the imaginative lavishness or the poetic structure of the original. On the contrary, it is trying to preserve the particularities of its writing, because, for example, the abundance of metaphors has a theatrical function – that of increasing the tension of speech and the energy of diction.

The problems of Shakespearian translation must not be thought of in terms of isolated words or lines, but in terms of the whole dramatic poem. Either the translated work is a poem as well, or else it is merely an explanatory and introductory paraphrase meant to decipher a complex text – and not to offer an imaginative and performable script.

There are always losses, passages which have a narrower scope than the original, but there can be successful inventions which make up for those losses. In French, Yves Bonnefoy's phrase, 'le tumulte de vivre', 'the turmoil of living', is a beautiful recreation of 'this mortal coil', in Hamlet's 'we have shuffled off this mortal coil'. Of course, only one meaning for 'coil' has been translated, that of turmoil, leaving out the quibble upon 'coil', the winding of a rope. But translation implies choices and in French, the phrase is extremely strong.

Translation has suffered far too long from a negative image. As George Steiner wrote: 'Attacks on the translation of poetry are simply the barbed edge of the general assertion that no language can be translated without fundamental loss. The postulate of untranslatability is founded on the conviction, formal and pragmatic, that there can be no true symmetry, no adequate mirroring, between two different semantic systems.' The sense of waste inherent in the concept of translation lies in the view which insists that the luminosity and pressure of the original text have not only been diminished by translation; they have been made to sound tawdry.

As Vladimir Nabokov expressed it in his poem *On Translating Eugene Onegin*,

> What is translation? On a platter,
> A poet's pale and glaring head,
> A parrot's screech, a monkey's chatter,
> And profanation of the dead.

Nabokov piles up negative images, ending with the charge of supreme sacrilege.

But the argument that each translation falls short is facile. No human product is perfect. No duplication even of materials that are essentially labelled as identical, will turn out to be a complete fascimile. Minute differences will always persist. To dismiss the validity of translation because it is not always possible, and never perfect, is absurd. Translation, in brief, is desirable and possible. We always have translated between languages, since the beginning of human history. The defence of translation in general starts with the immense advantage of fact. How can we go about our business, if the thing was not inherently feasible? Translation may be 'impossible', but so is all absolute concordance between thought and speech. Somehow the 'impossible' is overcome at every moment in human affairs.

Yet this pragmatic argument does not circumscribe the whole of the translator's experience, for, as soon as one defines translation as 'grasping a meaning', the fact that meaning is inseparable from the literal layer of speech immediately denies the legitimacy of that process. Translators, writers and readers have always experienced that. The conquering process of translation cannot be carried on without a certain feeling of violence, inadequacy and betrayal. Steiner again is right to talk of the sadness that always accompanies the experience of translation. There is always a certain element of pain, not only that of the translator, but, if I may say so, of the translated text – that is, of the meaning cut off from the letter.

Jacques Derrida describes this beautifully: 'The verbal body cannot be translated. Dropping that body is the essential energy of translation.' But what has been dropped, the body of the text, takes its revenge. Translation finds out to its cost that the meaning and the signifier are both dissociate and indissociate. In that sense, untranslatability is the life of speech. If in a text, the letter and the meaning are tightly linked, translation can only be a betrayal, even if this kind of betrayal is necessary for cultural exchange and communication in general. But the miracle is never complete. Each translation falls short. At best, translation can come close to the demands of the original, but there can be no total circumscription.

The truth is that the translator experiences at the same time the urge to translate and the impossibility of translation.

To quote George Steiner again:

Unquestionably there is the dimension of loss in translation, hence the fear of translation, the taboos which hedge sacred texts, ritual nomination . . . . But the residue is also, and decisively, positive.

The work translated is enhanced. This is so on a number of fairly obvious levels. Being methodical, penetrative, analytic, enumerative, the process of translation, like all modes of focused understanding, will detail, illumine and generally body forth its object . . . . The motion of transfer and paraphrase enlarges the stature of the original. Historically, in terms of cultural context, of the public it can reach, the latter is left more prestigious . . . . There can be no doubt that echo enriches, that it is more than shadow. The mirror not only reflects but also generates light.

Of course, some translations edge us away from the canvas, but others bring us up close. Such closeness is, of course, what every translator aims for – and tries to reach, humbly but with persistence.

Tindemans asked whether or not each generation requires its own translation of Shakespeare, 'as seems historically to have been the case', and a member of the audience, agreeing with Déprats, suggested that the very act of translation brought foreign directors and translators closer to the text than is customary in England, where we assume that we know what the text means. 'How long', she asked Alexander Anikst, 'will Pasternak's translations be valid?'

ALEXANDER ANIKST: The problem is a very important one. Jean-Michel Déprats has given us a brilliant argument, but I think it is a defeatist one, proving that there can be no accurate translation, which up to a point is true. Do we understand Sophocles, as he was understood in Athens in the fifth century BC? No. Do we understand Shakespeare, as he was understood at the Globe? Of course not. Art is a living thing.

This question is at the centre of modern aesthetics, the reception of works of art which modern theory proves is a very complicated process in which there are no absolutes. All that is absolute is that art is art and that it is beautiful. And every age tries to understand art, every nation tries to understand the art of other nations. And, of course, we put our Russian understanding into Shakespeare, just as you put your English understanding into Sophocles or Euripides. And so first of all I would suggest that real works of art are so great that any age can find beauty in them, their human value, their importance, in whatever language or social conditions they were originally created. We appreciate them, we understand them, they speak to us. That is the first and most important matter.

The second question is that modern theory has atomized knowledge. We dissect everything into small pieces, through semantics, semiology, matters of which I do not even know the correct names. But there is a reality beyond the dissection. *Hamlet* is a reality, *Othello* is a reality, *Romeo and Juliet*! You can feel them, you can understand them, they are live human images. When a translator does his job, he doesn't translate words, he re-creates the images. Will you believe me when I say that we have as great a *Hamlet*, an *Othello*, a *Macbeth*, as you English have?

My suggestion is that we need to study great works of art from all points of view, historically, linguistically, aesthetically, but we must not forget that there is a totality in works of art, and it is this totality which works upon us. That was what Pasternak meant when he said that his translation was an original piece of dramatic writing. He was only saying what other translators do, for they all try to re-create the work of art. Then comes the question, of course, as to what he has understood in the original work, and what he has managed to share in the translation, and what the spectators or the readers can gain from his efforts. But the matter is so complicated that we should not allow ourselves to become pessimistic.

Modern theatre, modern cinema and modern television recreate Shakespeare for the present generation – and for the future ones; and so we need to understand thoroughly the ways by which it is done and recognize that there is talent and genius in every job, including translation.

JEAN-MICHEL DÉPRATS: I think you misunderstood me. I was not being pessimistic at all. You can't deny that there are problems in translating Shakespeare. We are, of course, all trying to re-create the original. The question is: how do we go about it? There are some kinds of re-creation that are closer to adaptation or re-writing. Currently there is a demand in all countries for a closer text, which means not only fidelity to the original meanings but to the sounds as well, to whatever it is possible to achieve.

ERICH FRIED: It does translators no harm to study the meanings of the original and its background as closely as possible. But in the end, I don't think that I can translate Shakespeare because I've studied the original and read all the comments in the Arden Edition, but because I am a poet. You could feed all the facts about Shakespeare and his plays into a computer, and program the computer to translate – which has been done and the results were miserable. However scholarly and faithful a translation tries to be, the result has to be poetry, which is more than can be analysed.

This doesn't excuse translators who want to make life easy for themselves. In the Shakespearian line, 'Now the hungry lion roars and the wolf behowls the moon', one German translation substitutes 'tiger' for 'wolf', which is unforgivable, because it changes the nature of the forest: it becomes a jungle, where the characters can get eaten. There are similar howlers in all translations, but it is essential to remember that translation is an art in itself, and we often forget that fact.

JEAN-MICHEL DÉPRATS: But some poets keep close to the original, while others try to substitute their own poetics for those of Shakespeare. That has often been done, and these so-called poetic translations of Shakespeare often result in poor versions which date quickly. Great translations do not age – Luther's translation of the Bible, for example.

ERICH FRIED: It may not age, but there are a lot of mistakes in it.

An actor in the audience asked about the problem of topical jokes in Shakespeare. He had played the Porter in *Macbeth*, who makes three jokes, each with specific references to matters of the day which have now been forgotten. His director had not allowed him to change these contemporary allusions to bring them up to date. He was stuck with lines about 'the farmer that hang'd himself on th'expectation of plenty', the 'equivocator' and 'the tailor', and he had had to resort to mime to make these jokes funny. He would have preferred to have changed the jokes.

'This is where', said Déprats, 'you are better off with a translation, because you are not hampered by topical allusions. That particular speech translates very well. It can be very funny, whoever the equivocator may be. I translated equivocator by Jesuit.'

'That's because', replied the actor, 'the equivocator was a Jesuit, wasn't he? Isn't this a direct reference to the Gunpowder Plot?' 'Yes,' answered Déprats, 'but the reference is lost for a modern audience.' 'But', persisted the actor, 'weren't you tempted to make a similar joke, about the bombings in Paris, for example?'

JEAN-MICHEL DÉPRATS: No, I never alter the fabric of a text by contemporary topical allusions. Furthermore I don't think that the reference is all that important, although it may have been for Shakespeare's audiences. This raises the problem of cultural references. For me, that is not the most difficult kind of problem. An exact and poetic translation into French of Claudio's phrase in *Measure for Measure* where he describes life as 'this sensible warm motion' is much more difficult than the Porter's speech. Even puns are less of a problem, because in a way you are more free in translation to find some substitute to replace a pun that doesn't come across in modern English.

ERICH FRIED: I disagree slightly, because when a topical joke or pun doesn't come across in English anyway, we are not obliged to rescue it in translation. If I simply know what the meaning of the joke originally was, somehow this knowledge goes into me when I translate. If I am a good poet, and in the right mood, I find some solution. Translating is much less of a theoretical activity than it sounds. It has its own momentum, its own ecstasy.

Martin Esslin in the audience commented on the 'optimism' of Anikst's remarks.

MARTIN ESSLIN: It is possible to recreate Shakespeare in France and Russia because we have all had in our history the experience of kingship, feudalism, serfdom, and revolutions. But, as a translator, I think that it is mistaken to suppose that you can divorce the human substance of works of art from the historical contexts of language and culture in which they are embedded. Pasternak was in a fortunate position with Shakespeare, because he was still in the same Western tradition. If you translate modern works, you run up against the difficulty that our institutions in a divided world are so different that it is almost impossible to find equivalents.

You can sometimes get round the problems. For example, I translated a play by Harold Pinter where there is a long passage about cricket, but what he is actually talking about is sex. You know, this woman has wonderful footwork and she bowls these lovely googlies, and so on. And there's absolutely nothing that you can do to re-create that exactly. And so I phoned up Pinter and said, 'Will you allow me to translate this into soccer?' This was possible because I could write 'She dribbled through nicely and scored so many goals'. But if Pinter had written about a set of concepts, like the rules of cricket, for which there was no adequate substitute, then there is absolutely nothing that can be done. The humanistic optimism which states that everything is translatable into everything else is simply not true, for there are societies which have institutions and even biological differences that just cannot be translated. You can only write a commentary. I suppose that, under those circumstances, if you want to do a translation, you can go into the deeper structures of the text, and then find your way out again; but that is very difficult. I don't think that one should be too optimistic.

I have the experience as someone who speaks several languages fairly well, of teaching in America, where nobody knows any language at all any more; and the students are convinced that if you're taking a course in *The Divine Comedy* in translation, you are getting *The Divine Comedy*. They think that translation is a kind of sausage machine where you put the thing in one end and it comes out the other. But *The Divine Comedy* has innumerable references to people which you can't understand without a commentary, it has an extremely intricate metre which makes all the difference because it has mystical connotations and it tells you the time by astronomical scholarship that hardly anybody knows.

The great advantage of Shakespeare is that we *do* share the same set of historical concepts, a similar European background, and so it is still possible to do a good translation of Shakespeare. But we may well reach a moment in history when this situation is no longer possible. Indeed I think that in some parts of America it is impossible today.

'We may have shared something once', added Erich Fried, 'which we have now forgotten. Look at the falconry terms in *Othello*. What do people nowadays remember of falconry? Though it was once common to all European Christians.' 'But', insisted Martin Esslin, 'there is still falconry in France and probably in Russia. We all know something about it.'

'I know what you mean', said Déprats. 'I once had to translate a play by David Storey, *In Celebration*, and it was tremendously difficult. As with Martin Esslin's example of cricket, there are some things which you cannot translate. You have to adapt. What do you do, for example, with a Northern accent? Do you try to make these characters speak Northern French? That's a bad solution, but what do you do?'

'You have to make them speak something', said Fried, 'that is palpably a vernacular, but not a vernacular at home in any particular period. I had to do that with my translation of *Under Milk Wood*.' 'Brecht saw that', Esslin commented, 'as inventing a language that sounds like ours, but isn't!'

In the audience was Alfred Emmett, a founder member of the International Amateur Theatre Association, whose enthusiasm for the theatre largely helped to build the Questors Theatre in Ealing. 'In England', he said, 'we have many great difficulties with Shakespeare – trying to understand the language, having a long Shakespearian tradition and having audiences with preconceptions about how Shakespeare should be played. In one way, one can envy the freedom of those who translate Shakespeare into other languages. It's obviously essential that a Shakespearian translator has certain qualities. He has to be, first of all, a sensitive poet of the theatre. If he is one, then he may be able to create something which, in his own country, provides as good an interpretation as we often get here in England.'

'I like your phrase, "poet of the theatre"', said Déprats. 'Is there a difference between literary translations and theatrical ones? Professor Anikst gave an example of a good translation which, when it came to be acted, caused the actors to say, "It doesn't come across very well. We should change this and that!" I don't think that you can separate the two – but, historically, they have been separated, at least in French. Translation for the cultivated reading public: adaptation for the stage.'

'Certainly', added Fried, 'one mustn't translate Shakespeare as if he were a radio dramatist.'

ALEXANDER ANIKST: We have reached a point where several questions come together – and it's good that we have mentioned the translation of modern plays, because when we translate contemporary French, English, or American plays into Russian, we don't understand them very well, because we don't know that kind of life. And when you read Soviet plays, there are many things you wouldn't understand, because we have different life-styles. That is the general problem.

How is it solved? Great artists have found the solution. When we talk about modern plays, most of them are too naturalistic, too close to everyday life. The general human problems are wrapped in such clothing that the human element in them is not seen as it was in ancient art – and in Shakespeare, where humanity, what is understood by everybody, comes to the fore. Whether we know who the equivocator was or don't know, the Porter's scene creates a certain impression. We understand the deep meaning of it, although we don't know many things about Shakespeare's time. And so this turns the problem into the issue of what kind of art is now being created. Classical art – and I include both ancient Greek and Shakespearian plays in that category – has its appeal because certain human values are discussed there with such depth that unfortunately we do not find in contemporary plays.

MARTIN ESSLIN: That's true, but in Russian, English, French, and German civilizations, we have similar backgrounds. Everybody knows what a king is, or a weaver, or a moneylender. But when you get into societies with profound institutional and cultural differences, that common ground disappears.

Let me give an example. I was a BBC correspondent in Africa once; and I met a colleague who was just starting a native radio station in what is now Zambia. He told me that it was very difficult for certain plays to make sense to the audiences there, because they didn't have the same cultural pre-suppositions. There was a local play about a man who had a bicycle that he was very fond of, and he lost it. It was stolen. It became a kind of detective story. He tried one clue – nothing, second clue – nothing, third clue – nothing, fourth clue – nothing, fifth clue – nothing! Finally, the European producer said, 'What is the point of this play? It ends

– and he still hasn't found his bicycle!' 'You've got it all wrong', he was told. 'The point is that one shouldn't be too fond of one's bicycle!'

There you have an example of a play based on totally different assumptions which we could never do on the BBC because nobody would understand it, however brilliant and linguistically exact the translation.

'What about Eastern cultures?' asked Anikst. 'How can Chinese and Japanese poetry be translated? And yet it has been done. The French have made some beautiful translations of Chinese poetry.'

'So have the Germans and the English', answered Esslin, 'but they are completely different works of art. They are more than adaptations. They are variations on a musical theme, not the same composition.'

ALEXANDER ANIKST: I think we must add another important factor, apart from creativity – the human attempt to penetrate the cultural barriers. Our age is really one when we can begin to talk about a world culture. Our culture has been too Europeanized, too Westernized. We will have to start to understand Asian cultures, African cultures: we'll have to do away with our isolation.

This process has been going on between Western countries as well, and here we have already reached a certain level of understanding. The Germans claim Shakespeare as a German author. So do we. Chekhov is also an English author, Dostoievsky an American. We have come to a stage in human development when there is a necessity for closer study and closer understanding between nations.

Civilization has reached a very dangerous stage – and at the same time, a very hopeful one. If culture wins – culture and peace and understanding – then humanity will win. We'll do away with the barriers and the translators will do important work in bringing the nations together with common human values.

ERICH FRIED: Which must not be the lowest common denominator.

'Have there been', Anikst asked Carlos Tindemans, 'any good translations of Shakespeare in your country?' 'In Flanders?' Tindemans replied, carefully making the distinction between the Walloons (French-speaking

60

Belgians) and the Flemings. 'No, not as a complete Shakespeare. We learned Shakespeare in the Low Countries through French adaptations. Ducis, who adapted Shakespeare for the Théâtre-Français in the second half of the eighteenth century and incidentally didn't speak English at all, was the one who gave us our first Shakespeares and only in this century have we started to tackle the problem of providing our own Shakespeares.'

'Do translators', asked a member of the audience, 'observe the verbal structures that Shakespeare gave as an aid and indication to the actors?' He cited two examples from *Romeo and Juliet* – from the balcony scene, where several mid-line endings lend a spontaneous feeling to Juliet's speech, and Mercutio's Queen Mab speech, which is constructed in perfect iambic pentameters to give the impression that here is someone who is making a speech, as opposed to simply speaking. 'Yes', said Fried and Déprats simultaneously.

Another speaker praised foreign productions of Shakespeare, saying that sometimes they provided a more complete realization of the text than was normal in Britain. 'I can think of the *Macbeth* that the Toho Company from Japan brought to the Edinburgh Festival last year. I don't know a word of Japanese but I knew utterly and throughout that this was *Macbeth*. I saw an Iranian studio production of *Romeo and Juliet*, and again was deeply moved by the story in a language of which I know nothing. In Britain, we have the great advantage of having actors who can speak the verse and find their way past the words which, on the page, might mean absolutely nothing to us; but as a great speech rolls by, you can feel it totally, with every nuance. In the theatre, we have the aids of the director and the actors giving extra flesh to the speech – at least, they should be aids. You do not worry about what this word exactly means or whether it is the correct word. The actors can make it the correct word.'

Razak Ajala from Nigeria, in the audience, asked whether a line could be drawn between translation, adaptation and transposition. 'Processes of adaptation', answered Déprats, 'are always found in translation, particularly when you have to substitute one pun for another. Usually though the difference between a translation and an adaptation is clear-cut. In an adaptation, there are added passages and cut passages and passages where the poet substitutes a whole network of images for which there is no basis in the original. It may not always be easy to draw the line, but when Ducis made the hero die offstage, in accordance with Neo-Classical theory, that clearly was an adaptation.'

CARLOS TINDEMANS: At the core of modern translation theory is the recognition that an exact equivalent in a foreign language is an unreachable ideal. We may seek a desirable accuracy, but basically from the start of a translation, adaptation sets in.

As for adaptation for the stage, there is the example of Peter Zadek's *Othello*, which mixes up two different translations from different ages.

ERICH FRIED: And sometimes, when Shakespeare uses the same word in two different parts of the play, Zadek uses different words, because he hasn't noticed that the same words have been used. Zadek is a great director, but he has his weaknesses.

But in any case, we always assume that Shakespeare in his time had a more or less homogeneous audience that understood him in the same way. But I am sure that the old people and the young would have understood him slightly differently. Those involved with the fashions of the time would have understood his polemics against children's theatre – in *Hamlet*, for example – in a way which meant much less to others. That should encourage us.

Georges Banu in the audience asked Alexander Anikst what Shakespearian translations Chekhov would have used in *The Seagull*? 'He could have used six or seven translations, or even mixed translations which were very popular in Russia at that time', said Anikst. 'The character of Hamlet was always present in Chekhov's mind. He even wanted to write a Russian *Hamlet*, but not a direct adaptation.' Banu then asked about syntax. He pointed out that Anikst had talked about the different lengths of words in Russian and English, but said nothing about the structure of the sentences. 'What kind of syntax does Pasternak use?'

ALEXANDER ANIKST: You should never try to imitate the syntax of another language. Translations have to be made in such a way that the language sounds typically national, so that it can be understood by the new audiences. Pasternak followed a long tradition of Russian translation to make the foreign text sound as if it is purely Russian. The old translators used to follow all the movements of the original phrase, which made it practically impossible to grasp the meaning when it was performed on the stage. But modern translators try to keep away from Shakespeare's sentence structures, to make it sound like normal speech and not a translation. The same may apply to German translations, but there are many words in German which are more similar to the English. In German, for example, you have the article, whereas in Russian you don't have the article.

ERICH FRIED: Any translation that sounds like a translation is not a very good one. That applies in any language. But sometimes, almost by an Act of Grace, you discover that there is more in common between the different languages than you had thought possible. You can suddenly achieve a *verbatim* translation where you least expect it. But that only happens rarely.

*

Fried also mentioned the example of a German translator who had tried to translate Shakespeare into sixteenth- and seventeenth-century German, but had failed because 'there were no parallels between English and German societies at that time'. As Esslin had pointed out, translation was possible within limits between societies which shared some kind of common heritage; but this did not apply to non-European countries, where none the less Shakespeare's plays are also translated and performed.

Languages are products of their societies, as Fried stressed in choosing pre-Industrial Revolution words to translate Shakespeare. But there are many other social differences which separate Shakespeare's London from our own, among them the Elizabethan treatment of women, the topic simultaneously under discussion in the main Young Vic theatre. As Tindemans pointed out in closing the session, 'the more answers are found, the more questions remain'.

SESSION 3

IS SHAKESPEARE SEXIST?

with
Caroline Alexander, Michael Bogdanov,
Anna Földes, Zeynep Oral, Sue Parrish
and, in the chair, Marianne Ackerman

Katharine's last speech from *The Taming of the Shrew* was once a popular subject for samplers, and eight-year-old girls would embellish these lines, stitch by stitch:

> Such duty as the subject owes the prince,
> Even such a woman oweth to her husband;
> And when she is froward, peevish, sullen, sour,
> And not obedient to his honest will,
> What is she but a foul contending rebel,
> And graceless traitor to her loving lord?
>
> (V.ii.155)

But these sentiments were not Shakespeare's final words on this subject, and even in *The Taming of the Shrew*, they form part of a play within a play, staged before the astonished eyes of Christopher Sly, a drunken rogue who is kicked out of a pub by the landlady.

The ambivalence of Shakespeare on this question, as on many others, has always confused later admirers and critics. With other writers of his time, he shared a familiar Elizabethan technique, which was to take opposite extremes and present them side by side, inviting the audience to seek a middle way between them. If one extreme wins over the other, the result is often tragedy. If a balance is found, the end is harmony, love and, in a Shakespearian sense, comedy. In *The Taming of the Shrew*, the extremes are clear. Katharine the shrewish rebel becomes, after some rough handling, Petruchio's submissive wife and the result is not tragedy, but harmony. Katharine recommends submission to all other women.

The Taming of the Shrew has always been a popular play, but at different times and places, it has been presented either as good marriage guidance or as a skilful send-up of male chauvinist dreams. Which did Shakespeare really mean? The answer could lie in Shakespeare's other plays. There are many passages elsewhere in which submission in marriage is praised, together with those qualities which accompany obedience, such as a soothing voice and a reluctance to answer back. 'Her voice was ever soft', said Lear over the dead body of his daughter Cordelia. 'Gentle, and low – an excellent thing in woman.'

But Cordelia, of course, is someone who did answer back; and Beatrice in *Much Ado About Nothing* is another exception to the submissive rule. Beatrice's quick wit, however, is thought to be an obstacle to marriage. For both men and women, marriage is assumed to be the natural social state, involving a sacrifice of personal independence, but, for women, this loss of freedom is nearly total. They are reared as children towards marriage and have few other options. Their formal social duty is initially towards their fathers, who select their future partners, and then to their husbands. Shakespeare gives many examples of those who, like Juliet, rebel; but he also warns against wilfulness and disobedience. Even Portia in *The Merchant of Venice* is obedient to her dead father's wishes.

In this discussion we wanted to examine whether Elizabethan marriage customs and Shakespeare's treatment of women constituted a major barrier to our contemporary understanding of his work. In the chair was the Canadian critic of the *Montreal Gazette*, Marianne Ackerman, who began by ruling out of order speculation about Shakespeare's private life. She did not want the debate to be sidetracked into theories that he was really a homosexual and must have had an unhappy marriage, because he left Ann Hathaway in his will the second-best bed. 'We only', she said, 'have the enigma of his writings.'

MARIANNE ACKERMAN: I asked Jan Kott what he thought about this subject and he said, 'For 450 years, we talked about Shakespeare being sexy and now, for the last fifteen, he's sexist!' Is this just one of today's fashionable pre-occupations? I asked some colleagues, and they replied either 'Of course not, he's a genius' or 'Of course he's sexist, but he's a genius'; and in both cases, they thought that there was nothing more to discuss.

What interests me is not whether Shakespeare was sexist or not (whatever that may mean), but whether a contemporary woman can find herself or be found in Shakespeare's plays. Our problem of interpretation is not simply that of understanding the text, but also of seeing how that text connects with the life outside the theatre, in the streets, in our homes. Can women today relate to Shakespeare's plays and see their own lives in the circumstances he presents? If they can, we will have gone some way towards proving that, in this respect, he is our contemporary.

Marianne Ackerman turned to a founder director of the Women's Playhouse Trust, Sue Parrish, who is also a well-known free-lance director; and asked her whether Shakespeare was sexist.

SUE PARRISH: The short answer is 'Yes' and the longer answer is 'Yes', and there is a full discussion of this question in Marilyn French's *Shakespeare's Division of Experience*.

I think that there is a fundamental inequality and difference in the way in which Shakespeare treats his male and female characters. This inequality does have a powerful effect not only on women in the audiences, but also on the actresses who play his women.

I was brought up in a girls' school and always played men's parts in Shakespeare because I had a deep voice and was considered the best actress. This was very lucky because the men have the best parts. It was an interesting litmus test, for it was recognized without question that the male parts *demanded* the best actors. I did once play Goneril professionally, and that was not a happy experience. It was not just because she was not the centre of the play, but because there was some inherent human cruelty within her that had no root or psychological explanation. She isn't a person in the same sense that Lear is.

When you are an actress, you realize that in Shakespearian companies, women are outnumbered six, seven, eight times to one. This is accepted as a fact of life; and somebody even told me the other day that this reflects the outside world. Well, of course, it doesn't. In the outside world, there are 53 per cent of women to 47 per cent of men.

It is not just in numbers that men have a superiority over women in Shakespeare's plays. The female characters are, in general, powerless to influence the outcome of events; and because they are powerless, they are presented more as types than characters. If you talk to actresses, you will realize that they all share the experience in rehearsal of being isolated within male companies and are not able to play their full part in putting the production together.

Most directors are male and men have been trained from

childhood to grab as much attention as they can; and so in the actual rehearsals for Shakespeare's plays, women are at a disadvantage. That is our lot and our conditioning, which in Shakespeare reflects the whole background of the Christian tradition and the Bible; and you know what kind of roles women play in that particular story!

Marianne Ackerman turned to the French theatre critic of the Paris papers, Le Matin and La Vie française, Caroline Alexander.

CAROLINE ALEXANDER: I've been a critic for twenty years and I've never asked myself the question as to whether Shakespeare is sexist – and I'm a woman! The fact that I haven't thought about it is in itself revealing, because if he had been a terrible male chauvinist, I would have asked this question and probably rebelled against Shakespeare because of it.

On the contrary, for many years, I have always envied Shakespeare's female repertory. He is the only classic author whose plays show such an immense variety of roles for women, and here I disagree with Sue Parrish. They are characters, not types. I have always envied their importance in the action – and the fact that they are leading personalities, often providing the keys to the plots.

In France, we don't have the equivalent. Just compare our two superstars, your Shakespeare and our Molière, who is a little bit younger, only three hundred years our contemporary, instead of four hundred.

Of course you can say that in Shakespeare, women rarely have the title roles or, if they do, they share it with men. Of course, in Shakespeare, you can say that women remain dependent on men and that only men hold power: that may be true, *formal* power. Of the real power in action, well, I'm not so sure. Of course, Shakespeare was a witness of his times and he could not guess what would happen in the future; but that is no reason to suppose that he simply belongs to the past. If that were so, we would simply have forgotten him.

In Shakespeare, women belong to the upper classes, to the lower classes, to nobility, to history, to legends and fairy stories. They often share power, including political power, with men. In Molière, on the other hand, women belong to the middle classes, the up-and-coming bourgeoisie, or those who serve the bourgeoisie, their wives, their daughters who are always to be married off, their servants and peasants. The female power in Molière is strictly limited to the family circle and love affairs. Shakespeare presents each female character as an entire human being, without any particular classification, because they are all so different. They are what they are, with their own qualities, skills, defects, and failures.

But to our eyes, at the end of the twentieth century, Molière seems to divide women into two categories. On one side, there are the foolish, the silly, and the pretentious; on the other, the reasonable, sensible, and common-sensical. It's a simplifying process, which reveals Molière's fondness for ordinary people, the lower classes. In Molière, the more women try to rise in the traditional hierarchy, the more they make themselves look ridiculous. If they keep within the rules of etiquette, then Molière admires them and they become founts of wisdom and commonsense. They have to stay where they are, submissive, and then perhaps they can become clever, sensitive, clear-minded, and charming, or even a kind of rebel with a cause, like Agnès in *L'Ecole des Femmes*.

But I don't want to criticize Molière because he was fighting in his time against some old religious rules and conventions stemming from the Middle Ages. He was never a feminist, of course, but he was a revolutionary in that he was on the side of the young against the old, against selfishness and for boys and girls in love. But his aim was to please his audiences. He wanted to make them laugh, which was why he used caricatures. He did create some universal female characters with great psychological depth, but that does not make him a feminist.

But what about Shakespeare? His heroines are like kaleidoscopes. You look through them and you can turn them around to receive different images. Was Cressida only a coquette without a soul or, as Jan Kott has argued, the first modern feminine character? Some eight years ago, I was at Stratford to see the first performance of Michael Bogdanov's *The Taming of the Shrew* and I loved it. Bogdanov didn't change anything in the text or the spirit. He just had this wonderful idea of making Katharine into an intelligent woman who falls in love and compensates for Petruchio, the sort of rebel teenager whom a woman has to treat like a child. The situation was turned inside out – but it was simply an emphasis of interpretation.

Peter Brook said this about acting, that when he changes one performance in a play with twenty actors, he has to change the whole, because the relationships alter. And so, if Katharine just smiles, a slight smile, when she speaks the line, 'Such duty as the subject owes the prince, Even such a woman oweth to her husband', the relationships change completely. She knows what she is doing, she is being clear and is, in the end, in charge of the situation.

One final point. When Shakespeare wants to give his heroines a leading part in the action, he often dresses them up as men so that they can act like men, as in the cases of Portia, Viola, and Rosalind. Of course, one explanation could be that young boys were playing female roles and when boys dress as boys, everyone believes in them. That might have been the only reason, the conventions of the time. But there could be another explanation. We could give Shakespeare the credit of wanting to prove that when women dress like men, they can behave like men and be as clever as Portia in *The Merchant of Venice*.

Shakespeare was the first to realize that in every woman there is some characteristically male behaviour; and in this sense, he was closer to Freud and three hundred years or so ahead of his time. Shakespeare gave to literature and the theatre dominant female personalities, archetypes of good and evil, and of many different kinds of behaviour – which still exist. As to whether he was sexist or not, I don't care.

Marianne Ackerman asked the director, Michael Bogdanov, whether it was possible ever to direct *The Taming of the Shrew* as anything other than a sexist play. What was his interpretation in the RSC production, to which Caroline Alexander referred?

MICHAEL BOGDANOV: It was based on a theory that this is, in fact, a play about a male wish-fulfilment dream of revenge upon women. The humiliation to which Kate is subjected is what happens in a world ruled and dominated by men, where any woman who challenges male supremacy has to be smashed down by any means possible, until she is submissive, pliant and occupies her rightful place in the world, which is to warm the slippers, cook the meals and come when called.

From my point of view, this is not a theory so much as a revealing of the text. The induction expresses this clearly. A drunken tinker is thrown out of a pub by the hostess for smashing her glasses. As he lies on the ground, he says, 'I'll get my revenge on you!' and she says, 'I'll call the police' and he says, 'I don't care' – and falls asleep. From the darkness, comes a group of huntsmen, betting on their dogs. They see the drunken tinker lying there and they play a trick on him, still in his dream. In his dream, he becomes a lord, because if you're a drunken tinker, the one thing you envy is power, wealth, acquisition. You want to wive it wealthily in Padua and if you find a girl who is apparently defying the conventions of the time, and refusing to conform to the pattern as to how good little girls should behave, you say, 'That's the one, she's rich, and if she gives me a bad time, I'll smash her to the ground.' The other one, meanwhile, Bianca, 'the prize' as she's termed in the list of characters, is being held to ransom. She is being bartered to the highest bidder, handed to Gremio, Hortensio, and Tranio, in the place of his master, Lucentio, all vying to see which will have her hand in marriage.

This is the crux of the question. Can Shakespeare be a humanist – and sexist? For me, the two things are incompatible. You cannot believe in an egalitarian society, where might is not right, and still think that women should be abused and maltreated. In each of Shakespeare's plays, women are placed in a position where they have to fight to stay somewhere with some power if they do not want to slide down the slippery pole, like Margaret in *Richard III*. Shakespeare lays the blame at the door of society for the way in which women are treated. In *Romeo and Juliet*, a girl tries to make a choice of her own. The acquisitive Capulets say that she must marry Paris, kinsman to Prince Escalus, and therefore another rung up the social ladder. She

70

says, 'No. I want to marry – but Romeo.' By insisting that she should choose for herself, she denies the authority of her parents, and the Church abdicates responsibility, the Nurse abdicates responsibility and finally the two kids die, because this is a society which believes that women should be sold to the highest bidder.

And what do the two families do in the end? They vie with each other as to which can build the bigger statue in gold to the memory of their children. Still the acquisitive society! The only way in which you can measure human suffering, compassion and affection is in pillars of gold!

And so the same theory appears in *Romeo and Juliet* as in *The Taming of the Shrew*. It is the acquisitive society which is to blame, aided and abetted by the Church. You will remember the scene where Romeo says to the Apothecary, when he buys poison with gold, 'I sell thee poison, thou hast sold me none.' That is the real poison in the world, the poison in men's minds, gold, greed. It is gold and greed that makes men behave as they do to women, and makes men behave as badly to men as well. Shakespeare describes the ruthless pursuit of power, in which men and women get carved up.

Women are analysed in terms of having to stay close to the sources of power, if they want to survive, which is why Gertrude in *Hamlet* has to marry another king, the stronger man. Bianca, as soon as she gets the ring on her finger in *The Taming of the Shrew*, says to Lucentio, 'More fool you for betting on me!' That's what happens in the play. Men bet on women, as they bet on dogs; and so you find in Shakespeare the cyclical pattern of a society which, while apparently protecting women, actually batters them to pieces, and there is no doubt in my mind as to what Shakespeare's views on this matter were.

The next speaker was the author, theatre critic, and editor from Budapest Dr Anna Földes, whose thirteen books on Hungarian literature and politics include essays about, among other matters, the role of women in society.

ANNA FÖLDES: Sarah Bernhardt was not the only actress who fought against, and with, the female roles in Shakespeare. Our greatest nineteenth-century Hungarian actress, Mari

Jászai, did so as well. She played Portia, Lady Macbeth, Cleopatra and so on, but she also dreamt about playing Hamlet. It is a theatrical commonplace that Shakespeare didn't handle actors and actresses equally: you can't compare the part of Desdemona with that of Othello. The only exception to this rule is *The Taming of the Shrew*.

Despite this fact, I have to confess that, like Caroline Alexander, I was surprised and shocked to find in Canada a special chair of so-called Women's Studies and again at an International Symposium in Budapest that distinguished experts on the history of literature were examining classical and contemporary works from a feminist point of view. I could hardly imagine that it would be my task to study how Shakespeare's views correspond with our actual opinions about the social role of women. At the same time, I felt the challenge of accusing Shakespeare, and defending him against the more extreme charges. The examples are close enough to hand: it is just a matter of confronting them.

The most cruel and guilty heroine in Shakespeare is Hamlet's mother, Gertrude. The problem here goes beyond that of the individual portrait, for Hamlet is ready to generalize about her sins and faults. His monologue, 'Frailty, thy name is woman!' is an accusation and a judgement against the whole sex. This hatred is reflected later on when Hamlet denounces Ophelia.

The only other woman ranking with Gertrude to deserve her place in hell is Lady Macbeth. Mari Jászai first played Lady Macbeth very early on in her career when she was only 22, and when she was at the end of her career, she wrote about her reconciliation with the part. She said that at the beginning she hated the woman so much that she tried to reveal her pitiless ambitions at every moment when she was on stage. But she described the scene where the new royal couple remain alone with the crown, wordless and silent with fear, and she could give no explanation for the sudden silence.

Twenty-five years later, she played the part again and discovered that, behind the silence, lay the fact that Lady Macbeth does not accuse her husband who had promised her the crown. This shows a certain dignity and generosity

– and that she is prepared to accept a great part of their common crime. When she catches sight of Macbeth's breakdown, suddenly she collapses. She is not able to carry and bear the weight of that crime, because she's not used to it. When she planned and committed all these crimes, the actress explained, she didn't really know herself. She didn't suspect that she was not wicked enough. This scene, where she loses the moral balance in her soul, proves that here was a quality which she had once possessed. When she cries out for lost innocence and purity, this demonstrates how far she has fallen, which someone who has never been innocent, could not imagine.

And so Lady Macbeth is not just a stereotype of a wicked woman, nor is Gertrude, of course. But they are not the only daughters of Shakespeare. There are so many of them, Juliet, Volumnia, Portia – and the second Portia in *Julius Caesar*, who asks her husband, Brutus, about his worries and problems, insisting that she is not a concubine but a wife, entitled to know. There may not be a word about equality or partnership, but that example in itself should deny the suggestion that Shakespeare is a sexist.

As for *The Taming of the Shrew*, the key lies in the last monologue of Katharine where, traditionally, she gives up her independence to obey her husband for ever. There is, however, another interpretation. In 1976, Harry Levin predicted in his book, *Shakespeare and the Revolution of the Times*, that after a Beckett *King Lear* and Jonathan Miller's colonialist *The Tempest*, there could be an adaptation of *The Shrew* as a parable of women's lib.

Well, that had already happened. One of the first feminist *Shrews* took place in a suburban theatre in Budapest in 1974. The director succeeded in altering the conflict and the conclusion of the play. Even the set was unusual. It was composed of gold chains suggesting the golden prison of marriage. Instead of the normal induction scene, the director opened the play with the closing monologue, as a statement about marriage and about accepting the traditional passive role in marriage as a lively young girl might do, enthusiastically, hopefully, but also ironically. Later on, as in the text, the monologue was repeated, but the meaning was different. Kate's confession sounded like a bitter, hopeless protest song. Kate, as she gave herself up, was lost, even her fancy red dress was gone, together with her smile.

That was how it ended, with the image of her pale face and grey dress; and beneath them, we felt all the lost illusions and the modern, bitter, feminist message.

The last platform speaker was the Turkish author and theatre critic for the national daily, *Milliyet*, Zeynep Oral, who is also one of the few feminist writers in the region. Her first book, *To Be a Woman*, published in 1986, was an outright best-seller, while her second, published in the same year, *A Voice*, based on an interview with a woman in prison, sparked off a major political controversy. She began by describing what it is like to live in Turkey.

ZEYNEP ORAL: Turkey is a Muslim country, geographically between Asia and Europe, to the West of the Middle East and the East of East Europe, in the middle of many things. Economically, we call ourselves a 'developing country', because it is impolite to say 'underdeveloped'. Politically, we are a democracy, with military coups every ten years or so, and, on paper, women's rights, every one that you can think of, were granted to us sixty years ago, much earlier than in the West, and are enshrined in our Constitution.

But these rights are on paper. No woman ever lifted a finger to secure those rights. Some take them for granted, very few try to put these rights into practice in everyday life and some merely disregard them. Many even do not know that they exist.

We do not have such a developed Shakespeare industry as in the West. In the early 1920s, when Shakespeare was first staged, Muslim women were forbidden to go on the stage. The women's parts were either acted by men or by Christian women living in Turkey. This year, we had a production of *The Taming of the Shrew*, and even in Turkey, it's hard to swallow the kind of speech that Katharine has to make at the end of the play. Some Turkish women do believe that their husbands are lords, governors, sovereigns of their lives, but they don't go to the theatre. The ones who do, with their husbands, are more up to date; and in a civilized society, you cannot accept these statements about the role of women in marriage very easily.

Yücel Erten, one of Turkey's most talented young directors, turned the play into a tragedy. I'll just describe the
final scene and indicate how he got to it. Kate arrives at that
banquet with a huge shawl around her hands and arms. She
speaks that final diatribe of submission, and puts her hands
on the floor, and offers herself to her husband. But she has
cut her veins, and dies.

How did he arrive at that tragic ending, which may have
been the complete opposite of what Shakespeare intended?

First of all, like Michael Bogdanov, he stressed that this
was a world dominated by power, money and men. The
shrewishness of Kate is not part of her nature. She is an
intelligent girl who builds up this shrewishness as a shell to
protect herself from the domination of the outside world.
With that shell around her, she can be very strong. When
Petruchio, that crazy man, comes in, she can run away, and
she builds other shells to protect herself; but she falls in love
with Petruchio. That's when her tragedy starts. The shell
shatters.

In that scene where they return to her father's house, and
she is forced to swear that the sun is the moon, you can feel
that Kate is going through a kind of breakdown, the start of
the tragedy. For audiences who had never seen or read *The
Taming of the Shrew*, this production was a revelation.
They loved it. They thought it was the most marvellous play
they had ever seen and they identified with Katharine's fate.

The critics were more divided. Feminism has different
connotations in different parts of the world and at different
times of the century; and even within Turkey, there were
contrasting views between different feminist groups. Some
extreme ones loved this ending, saying that it was a form of
protest against the traditional conclusion. I didn't myself
agree, nor was I happy with the ending, for I don't think
that suicide is a protest against anything but life itself.

Members of the audience wanted to intervene. One challenged Sue Parrish
to explain what she meant by the inadequacy of the female roles in
Shakespeare. Weren't they in fact rather good?

SUE PARRISH: Let's take Lady Macbeth as an example. I'm sure that most people would think it a great part to play, but actually, it's quite a small part, in terms of lines and time spent on stage. The play is mostly concerned with men deciding what should happen.

We're all agreed that Shakespeare was a genius, but also a man of his time. As a genius, he developed as an artist throughout his life, and his attitude towards women is always changing. But as a man of his time, he pays more attention to the roles that men play in society than women, which is why modern women can find only two or three people on the stage with whom they can identify.

And these two or three female characters are constricted in their experiences. They do not have the same ability to be as fully human as the men. They aren't allowed to get angry or to be as much in error as the men. They do not learn by their experiences. The men do. They learn, they change. The men have the journey through the play.

There are also certain qualities in our society which are supposed to be male or female. We would probably, for example, place compassion at the female end of the spectrum, whereas aggression is a male characteristic. Shakespeare was concerned to make a synthesis between these opposites. Of course, he was concerned about the greed and power-grabbing in the world of his time; but he saw through its folly, calling on compassion, the feminine principle, to moderate it. But this synthesis is not expressed through the female characters, but the male ones. In *King Lear*, it is not Cordelia who reconciles the warring elements, but Edgar and Kent.

The questioner in the audience commented drily that if women in Shakespeare don't learn by experience, it was because they already knew the answers. 'Juliet, even as a child', she went on, 'knew that there could be fatal consequences to what she was doing. Beatrice in *Much Ado* knows all about the priorities in a relationship. It is Benedict who has to learn!'

'But is that true to life?' asked Sue Parrish, 'Were you born knowing everything?' 'Of course not', was the reply.

'That is partly what I mean', said Sue Parrish, 'women are idealized in Shakespeare. They still are in our contemporary culture. In plays written by men, it is women who carry the moral can. This is all part of the idealization of women which comes through the Christian tradition.'

'But are these important distinctions?' asked another member of the audience. 'I don't think that gender in itself is the crucial concept. There are more fundamental divisions in Shakespeare, between good and evil, and between male and female principles. Lady Macbeth has these very practical, awesome speeches where she asks for all which inhibits her from action to be stripped away. Specifically she denounces her female organs. "Come, you spirits, that tend on mortal thoughts, unsex me here!" At that moment, Shakespeare makes it clear that the forces for moral order in the world are part of what is called the female principle. The fact that it is a woman who is standing in front of the audience, denouncing her own nature, makes the image all the more powerful.'

'Whenever something particularly wicked is to be done', commented another speaker, 'the characters stress their maleness. "If it be man's work, I'll do it!" The same phrase crops up in so many plays, *Richard III*, *Macbeth*. It often means killing children. That's what men are good for, killing children.'

'All the characters in *Macbeth*', said a third member of the audience, 'subscribe to sexual stereotypes. When Lady Macbeth says, "Are you a man?" her image as to how a man should behave is different from Macbeth's. When Macduff hears the news of the death of his wife and family, Malcolm says to him, "Dispute it like a man!" and he replies, "I shall do so, but I must also feel it like a man."'

A speaker from the floor argued that all of Shakespeare's plays, but particularly *Macbeth*, represented a period of transition from a matriarchal society to a patriarchal one. He drew a parallel with Greek drama and pointed out the similarity between the witches in *Macbeth* and the Furies. 'The Witch', he said, 'is the pejorative, patriarchal, misogynist caricature of the White Goddess. In Elizabeth's reign, Shakespeare was very conscious of matriarchy. It is the struggle of transition that is so fascinating.'

Caroline Alexander stated that the bias against women is present throughout European literature and theatre.

CAROLINE ALEXANDER: In France, there are very few women directors and it was only about twenty years ago that women started directing at all. I have never found out why this is so. Even very famous women directors, like Ariane Mnouchkine, have no answer. They only say that perhaps they do not have the instinct for power or the opportunity to gain experience.

There are very few plays just for actresses, *The House of Bernarda Alba* perhaps, and a few other exceptions; and so there are not the same opportunities for actresses. Even in

movies, men have more chances to be extras or play bit
parts.

*

'This is why', said an actress in the audience, 'women feel at a disadvantage in rehearsals. We're so much outnumbered by men, particularly in
Shakespeare. When Harriet Walter was rehearsing for Ophelia in Richard
Eyre's *Hamlet*, with Jonathan Pryce, she had a difficult time in the nunnery
scene, where Pryce was insulting her and knocking her about, which is *not*
in the text. Harriet Walter complained that this violence made nonsense
of her lines which followed. Would she really under those circumstances
have called him "the glass of fashion and the mould of form"? And Harriet
Walter was told to sort out these problems for herself!

'That is a precise example of what Sue Parrish was describing. Actresses
are put on the sidelines in Shakespeare's plays and can't take part in the
interpretative process. They haven't got the most important roles and
Shakespeare often subjects them to unspeakable behaviour, as in *Othello*,
where all three women are reduced to whores. Nor, apart from Cleopatra,
are there many examples of sexually mature women. The role models
Shakespeare offers are those of victims, innocents, or whores; and these
stereotypes feed back into the rehearsal process, where actors and directors underrate the contribution of women, consciously or unconsciously,
because the play is encouraging them to take that view.'

The last speaker from the audience wanted to take Michael Bogdanov
to task. She was far from convinced by the theory that *The Taming of the
Shrew* was really a feminist play in disguise and thought that Zeynep
Oral's account of the Turkish production amounted to re-writing the play.
Wasn't this an example of directorial cheating?

She blamed Jan Kott for encouraging directors to take on board some
bizarre ideas, which might seem intellectually stimulating but actually ruin
the plays. She gave several examples. Kott had suggested that it was every
man's fantasy to see his wife seduced by an ass, which is why Oberon had
transformed Bottom. This silly notion was incorporated into Peter Brook's
A Midsummer Night's Dream. In *King Lear*, again under the influence of
Kott, Brook left out the passage where the servants prepare whites of egg
to bathe the bleeding eyesockets of Gloucester. That touch of humanity
did not suit their interpretation.

'Isn't it much easier', she asked, 'to pretend that Shakespeare *is* our
contemporary – and then distort what he has to say, rather than confront
the challenge of his actual meaning?'

'We should leave that question', said Marianne Ackerman, 'to the very
end of the conference.' And accordingly, she declared the session closed.

IS SHAKESPEARE STILL TOO ENGLISH?

with
Peter von Becker, Stavros Doufexis,
Anna Földes, Toby Robertson,
Yasunari Takahashi and, in the chair,
Kenneth Richards

Shakespeare's plays may be performed around the world, but in some respects they remain very English. There are many nationalistic and even jingoistic passages; and the French are not likely to applaud his treatment of Joan of Arc in *Henry VI (Part One)* or of Agincourt in *Henry V*.

In the patriotic 1940s, John of Gaunt's speech in *Richard II* was a standard elocution exercise,

> This royal throne of kings, this scept'red isle,
> This earth of majesty, this seat of Mars,
> This other Eden, demi-paradise,
> This fortress built by Nature for herself
> Against infection and the hand of war . . .
>
> (II.i.40)

and so on, for another fourteen lines; but by the subversive 1960s, such sentiments were deemed to be embarrassing. Comedians cracked jokes about 'this septic isle'.

Patriotism aside, Shakespeare's descriptions of climates and English landscapes can sound strange and exotic in other parts of the world. In the Negev desert, Arab students study Shakespeare at the Department of Seventeenth-Century English Literature at Beersheba University; and there winter is closer to the British spring, for it brings rain, whereas summer is the time of drought and death. When the students are confronted by a Shakespearian line like, from *Richard III*,

> Now is the winter of our discontent
> Made glorious summer by this Sun of York
>
> (I.i.1)

79

they can jump to the conclusion that the English are very odd, if not mad.

By itself, this line can be easily explained, but it is not so simple to express the metaphors which stem from Shakespeare's perception of the natural order of the universe (which may not be so natural elsewhere) and how it relates to human affairs, whereby the sun is the king and the clouds are those envious courtiers whose aim is to blot out the bounty of the sun and plunge the kingdom into darkness and disunity. Students can learn to analyse this kind of iconography, but it is a cerebral process, as ours would be if we tried to analyse the meanings of African masks. Seminars on geography are a poor way to approach Shakespeare's lyric poetry, which shimmers with pictures of the Warwickshire countryside.

> I know a bank whereon the wild thyme blows,
> Where oxlips and the nodding violet grows
> Quite over-canopied with luscious woodbine,
> With sweet musk-roses, and with eglantine.
> (*A Midsummer Night's Dream* II.i.249)

Shakespeare's knowledge of Europe and the Mediterranean is sketchy, although his plays are often set in Italy, France or Cyprus, or further afield, in Bohemia. But how do people who come from these countries respond to these Anglo-Saxon travel impressions? Can they find parallels in their own cultures to the Englishness of Shakespeare's world view? If they can't do so, then are they actually seeing Shakespeare's plays at all, or merely inkblot versions, on to which they can project their own outlooks?

The chair for this session was Kenneth Richards, Professor of Drama at Manchester University and Director of the University Theatre, who began by remarking upon the history of Shakespearian productions in Europe.

*

KENNETH RICHARDS: Yesterday we discussed the translation of Shakespeare's plays, but for a long time there was a gap between the first translations and their actual performances on foreign stages. In Italy, for example, the first translations were made in the mid- to late eighteenth century, but the plays weren't performed at least in fairly recognizable versions until the mid-nineteenth century. Indeed to speak of Shakespeare on the Continental stages at that time is somewhat misleading, for only a few of the plays were widely known and performed, and even fewer were noticeably popular. Guy Dumur pointed out yesterday that in France now Shakespeare is much more 'our contemporary' than he has ever before been, for there has never been a time when so many of his plays have been performed; and that is equally true for most other countries.

In the nineteenth century, the tragedies were by far the best known on the Continent, and only later was attention paid to some of the comedies and the Roman plays, while the English history plays remained for the most part inaccessible. It is only since the last war that the whole range of Shakespeare's work has been presented internationally with any regularity. Laurence Olivier's film of *Henry V* was perhaps the first post-war international Shakespeare success. Why was that? If its celebratory patriotism caught the mood of the times in England, that mood too seems to have been one with which other nations were able to identify. Perhaps, a little later, the influence of Brecht and the Berliner Ensemble changed our attitude towards the epic nature of the history plays. Perhaps too, since the war, the prominence of the director as opposed to the star actor, has encouraged the epic approach.

I have stressed the comparative neglect abroad until fairly recently of the history plays because it is in these that Shakespeare's chauvinism seems most apparent.

Kenneth Richards then turned to the British director, Toby Robertson, currently the artistic director of Theatre Clwyd in North Wales. During the 1970s, Robertson was best known as the director of the touring company, Prospect; but he also had wide experience in directing foreign companies, notably in China.

TOBY ROBERTSON: There have really been two sides to my work abroad. During the 1970s, Prospect toured a great deal for the British Council, but I have also directed in languages that I don't speak for companies overseas. It is always infinitely rewarding to do a Shakespearian play not in English and somehow it is much easier to direct. I get far less worried about every single detail.

When we went abroad with Prospect and performed in English, I was always careful to choose a play which had some relevance to the country we were visiting. When we went to the Middle East, we did *Pericles*, and visited the places mentioned in *Pericles*, with a score by Carl Davies that was Levantine in feeling. By chance, he wrote a tune that was exactly the same as a pop hit in the Levant at that moment! It went down well. We went to the Temple of Jupiter at Baalbek in the Lebanon with this androgynous *Pericles*, which was given the concept that it was being played in a brothel as a flashback to Marina's experiences; and somebody said that this was the first time the Temple of Jupiter had smiled, since the Mysteries were put down by Constantine. The androgynous sexuality of the production made the setting come alive again. This Levantine *Pericles* was something which people could understand in terms of the place.

Again, we performed *Twelfth Night* at Dubrovnik in an Illyrian setting. Again, music was very important. We found two people who played Illyrian instruments, and through music we capitalized on the ethnic quality of the setting. That was something which we always tried to achieve.

The other kind of experience is when one goes to direct a play in another country in a foreign language. Here, my most interesting experience was in China. Again the first question was to find the right play. I had already been to China with *Hamlet* with Derek Jacobi, which played in Peking and Shanghai; and I was asked to go back if we could find a suitable play. This was for 1981, and so the invitation must have come in 1980.

The effects of the Cultural Revolution, the turmoil and the bruising, were just beginning to fade. They were starting to perform Shakespeare again in China, and I remember seeing some of their productions. Their theatre was still a kind of off-shoot of the Peking Opera, highly fantastical, like a museum. You couldn't see anything modern about it at all. All Europeans in their productions were given an enormous amount of nose putty: they thought we all had big noses. The make-up actually came from a Leichner book of 1930. It was like walking back into the past, as I imagine a Daly production might have looked like at the old Gaiety.

We talked a long time about the choice of play and finally we decided upon *Measure for Measure*; and we were particularly lucky to have as our translator Stephen Ying, a fascinating man who had done the translation of *Hamlet* for Prospect. We couldn't call the play *Measure for Measure*. We called it *Three Men in a Vat*, which is part of a Chinese proverb similar in meaning to 'measure for measure'. I wanted to do the play in modern dress. The best productions of *Measure for Measure* I had seen were Jonathan Miller's studio version at the National Theatre and Stuart Burge's production, both of which caught the ironic comedy of the situation.

We had chosen *Measure for Measure* for one particular reason. The trial of the Gang of Four was looming over all China and nobody knew what was going to happen. There is one line in *Measure for Measure*, 'The law hath not been dead, though it hath slept' and I believe that this production was being used as a re-statement of the value of the law. In one way, it had a propaganda purpose.

I wanted to do it very simply in a convention which in the West we have all learnt to understand, basically in a black box. Well, we understood it then in the 1970s, although we have now moved towards something far more operatic in our sets and production styles. But we wanted to stage it simply, to strip the play down to its basic ingredients, which the Chinese actors found very odd in rehearsals. They would turn up with every single aid to acting that they could possibly use – hats, sticks, moustaches and false noses – to which I said 'No', and they were upset.

But we did strip it down to the ironic play that it is; and I came to feel that we had chosen a good play for China. Their sense of the ironic is very highly developed. I sometimes think that the older the civilization, the greater the sense of irony, which is why doing Shakespeare in the United States can be painful, because there is no sense of irony at all. I felt in the end that we had found something necessary for them – a theme that was contemporary, relevant and important.

One final point. I have often found that the history plays, oddly enough, are particularly exciting and revealing in foreign productions. I thought that the production by the Rustaveli company of *Richard III* caught something about that play which I have not seen elsewhere; and there was a production at the Gorki Theatre in Moscow of both parts of *Henry IV*, brought together into one evening. They paid the price of cutting out all the women's scenes totally – Mistress

Quickly, Doll Tearsheet, all had gone. But as an expression of a power struggle, and the mechanisms of power, it was supreme. It was, I suppose, influenced by Jan Kott. These were two of the most successful productions of the history plays that I have seen; and I have not felt that the Englishness was a barrier, if you can find the visual connections to make the play understood.

Kenneth Richards picked up this last point. 'Can this imaginative re-orchestration of the history plays displace the problem of the jingoism or chauvinism in Shakespeare, which some English critics feel to be strong and potentially offensive?'

'The themes are so universal', answered Toby Robertson, 'I have never found the Englishness a barrier.' 'Even in *Henry V*?' asked Richards. 'Well, yes, even there. It depends on how you treat *Henry V*. You can find parallels with some Japanese films, where you can find the same sense of martial glory, of jingoism. It depends, I suppose, on whether you want to laud jingoism or show how futile it is. But I don't think that *Henry V* is the very jingoistic play that the film suggests. Again, that is Shakespeare used for propaganda purposes.'

Kenneth Richards then turned to Yasunari Takahashi, asking whether he felt that for Japanese practitioners and audiences, Shakespeare was too distinctly English to be easily accessible? Takahashi is a Professor of Drama in Tokyo with a particular interest in Shakespeare.

YASUNARI TAKAHASHI: The history of the productions and translations of Shakespeare's plays in Japan sheds an interesting side-light on our culture as a whole. One of the first Shakespearian productions in Japan was a garbled Kabuki-style version of *Julius Caesar*, in about 1868, just after the Meiji Revolution; and it had a camouflaged message of political protest against the policy of the then reigning government, which was desperately trying to establish law and order and bureaucratic efficiency in a country newly opened out to the West. The modernization of Japan meant, naturally, Westernization.

The first full production of *Hamlet* in Tokyo's largest theatre, the Imperial Theatre (and the name, Imperial, is symbolic) came in 1911, with a very faithful translation by the great Shakespearian scholar Tsubouchi Shoyo, and it marked the beginning of the process of copying Western culture and society in general. It initiated the tradition in

Japan of Shakespeare in doublet and hose.

With Ibsen and Chekhov, Shakespeare became and continues to be one of the mainstays of Westernized theatre, which we name Shin Geki. Shin Geki literally means just 'modern theatre', but actually it denotes two things: (a) Western plays in translation, performed in Western costumes, sometimes with blond wigs and artificial noses, though fortunately this practice has virtually disappeared; and (b) Japanese plays about Japanese subjects, written in Western-influenced style by contemporary Japanese playwrights.

These mainstream Shakespearian productions were so prevalent that even some famous Kabuki actors were tempted to perform roles like Othello, Hamlet, or Macbeth. As you may know, in Japan, various forms of theatre art, such as Noh, Bunraku, Kabuki, and so on, are sharply separated from one another. This overstepping of the boundaries by the Kabuki actors was therefore rather unusual. But I must stress that even in these performances, the production was always in the Western style. There was no attempt to make Shakespeare Japanese.

Kurosawa's bold film adaptation of *Macbeth*, *The Throne in Blood*, in 1957, did not apparently influence stage Shakespeares at all. The doublet-and-hose tradition continued, uncritically, ostensibly faithful imitations of conventional Western Shakespeares, and it dominated the Japanese theatre until the late 1960s and early 1970s. That was the time of the students' revolt, when the younger generation provided a fundamental critique of Shin Geki and its West-orientated ideology of modernization.

I shall confine myself to mentioning only three instances of the new images of Shakespeare which emerged from this period.

The first is a group which called itself simply The Shakespeare Theatre, led by a young director, Norio Deguchi. All the actors in that company were in their twenties or early thirties at that time. They called their performances 'Shakespeare in Jeans' – or possibly T-shirts! Anyway, that's what they wore. They succeeded in bringing Shakespeare remarkably close to the contemporary Japanese sensibility of the young, including teenagers; and they achieved a record: they performed all thirty-seven Shakespeare plays during the seven years of their existence, until unfortunately they disbanded three years ago.

Another avant-garde company which should be mentioned is Scot, led by Tadashi Suzuki. Suzuki had shied away from Shakespeare after his *Macbeth* adaptation in 1973, until he challenged *King Lear* two years ago. This was just before the release of Kurosawa's *Ran*, but I don't think that Suzuki's all-male production had any influence on the film. Suzuki's *King Lear* is a brutally shortened adaptation, just like his recent adaptations of Chekhov's *Three Sisters* and *The Cherry Orchard*. He doesn't care a fig about the Englishness of Shakespeare, any more than he did about the Greekness of Euripides in his *Trojan Women*, performed in London at the Riverside Studios two years ago. With radical concentration, Suzuki extracts the essential components of *King Lear* and rearranges them. But the result is quite unlike the Charles Marowitz *Hamlet Now*, because Suzuki's characteristic stylization made it uniquely Japanese, at the same time as it universalized the themes of old age, fear, love, and hatred.

My last example may be familiar to some of you. The Toho Company's *Macbeth*, directed by Ninagawa, was seen in Edinburgh last year. It's a *tour de force*. Ninagawa transferred the whole setting to late sixteenth-century Japan, with Macbeth and the other characters clad in impeccable Samurai costumes and with petals of cherry blossom ceaselessly falling down on the stage like snow-flakes. It is all very Japanese and very picturesque and exotic.

But it is not simply a matter of visual beauty, but also of ethics. Macbeth's downfall looks here as if it has been lifted somehow from the realm of moral struggle, as in most Western productions, to that of sheer aesthetic life-style, or should I call it death-style, for Ninagawa's Macbeth, though he does not, of course, commit suicide, does seem to approach the highest ideal of the Samurai, *hara kiri*, as the supreme aesthetic act. The catharsis that an audience is meant to experience at the end of the play, despite the hero's villainy, seems easier to achieve in this Japanese

Macbeth than it usually is in an English one.

But what makes Ninagawa's *Macbeth* a *tour de force* is the fact that the text here is a very faithful translation. It's not an adaptation at all, except for slight changes in the place names, such as replacements of Ireland by the more vague 'Western Country' and England by 'Southern Country'. As far as language is concerned, this Samurai *Macbeth* sounds like other *Macbeth* productions in doublet and hose. It would be wrong to regard this *Macbeth* as simply a picturesque, operatic spectacle, devoid of linguistic significance. It is a measure of Ninagawa's great talent that the Japanese audience feels at home with the incongruity of Samurai pronouncing English proper nouns.

Ninagawa also had the boldness to frame the whole stage inside what is called a Butsudan, a Buddhist altar which can (or used to) be found in most Japanese houses and are the religious centres of daily life where the spirits of ancestors are supposed to dwell. And Ninagawa put a couple of old women on both sides of this huge Butsudan on stage, squatting, eating, knitting, and doing various everyday jobs during the performance of *Macbeth*. This scenic device made the whole action of *Macbeth* look like a play within a play and when the play ends, the old women, who look like Bedouins, close the doors of the Butsudan, which suggests that the tragedy has taken place inside that altar, inside the collective memory of the nation. And so the play acquires a religious dimension unknown in the original.

This proves, I think, that Shakespeare's theatre as an art form can take a great deal in its stride – and it is also a warning that the monopoly of this English treasure is being constantly threatened by talented directors from foreign countries.

Kenneth Richards asked Takahashi whether it was significant that all the plays he had mentioned were tragedies, and *Julius Caesar* a Roman play. 'In other words, precisely those plays that were first familiar abroad to Continental audiences? What about the Japanese attitude towards the comedies, like *As You Like It*?'

'I do remember', said Takahashi, 'some Japanese versions of the comedies. There was a *Much Ado About Nothing*, set in the revolutionary time when Westerners first came to Yokohama, which added an extra dimension of interest. They didn't tamper with the text, except with the names, which were turned into Japanese names. Essentially, though, it was a mainstream Shakespeare, that is, in imitation of Western Shakespeares.'

'Have any of Shakespeare's plays not been done in Japan?' asked Richards. 'Or only very rarely?' 'Well, there was the "Shakespeare in Jeans" company that did the lot', Takahashi answered, 'but otherwise there are about a dozen plays which have still never been performed in Japan in a major theatre.'

'I can remember', said Richards, 'seeing a production in Rome not so long ago of *Timon of Athens*, which was, I was told, only the second professional production it had ever been given in Italy. Some plays are very rarely performed on the Continent, let alone further abroad, in countries like Japan. Again Professor Takahashi has mentioned the brutally foreshortened *King Lear*. I can remember a similar treatment in Germany of *Othello*, which was like a cartoon: Othello had black roughly daubed on his face and Desdemona was a big, busty, sluttish blonde in fishnet tights and a suspender belt.'

Richards then asked the German theatre critic and editor of *Theater Heute*, Peter von Becker, whether he had seen that production and what he had thought of it.

PETER VON BECKER: Yes, that was an outstanding production in my view, and one of the truest to the original.

I have been sitting here thinking about whether this question makes much sense. There is only one thing which is too English for me and that's cricket. You can't understand cricket unless you've been English for 350 years. But otherwise I can't imagine any English topic or problem which isn't nowadays relevant for the rest of this modern, very small world.

Shakespeare himself played this game of time and countries. Of course, we know that his plays were written at a particular time and for the actors at the Globe Theatre; but they are also universal. Shakespeare's Rome, Athens, Venice, or Verona were never real geographical places. He had never been there. He invented them. We could turn this question around and ask whether Shakespeare is English at all? Did this England ever exist which he writes about even in his history plays?

Or alternatively, as a German critic, I could ask, 'Is Shakespeare too German?' As you know, there exists in Germany the longest tradition of Shakespearian translations, the most famous being the Schlegel/Tieck version which created a very Romantic image of Shakespeare which lasted for a long time. It was not a realistic Shakespeare, with all the levels of language from the language of kings to the language of whores. It was a middle level, but very poetic; and it established a tradition which has led on to today, where our major poets, such as Erich Fried or Heiner Müller, want to translate Shakespeare. Shakespeare is performed ten times more often every season in German-speaking countries than in English-speaking ones. I don't think that in any language Shakespeare is an author to be read in a train or an airplane; and for students, the baroque language on the page is quite difficult to understand. Shakespeare only lives when he is performed on the stage.

But can we talk about classics belonging to any country any more? The French have their classics, Racine, Corneille, and Molière, the Italians have Ariosto, Tasso, and Goldoni and their Commedia dell'Arte, the Spanish have Calderón and García Lorca – but they are really all part of a European theatrical tradition. In Germany, we sometimes ask the question, do we have drama today? Are there any real, contemporary dramatists at all? And in the eighteenth century, intellectuals were asking the same question, but in those days, they would have answered, 'Shakespeare'. Shakespeare was their great idol.

I think there are two main problems when we ask whether Shakespeare is too English – or our contemporary. We have to get back what Brecht called the sense of history. If you try to actualize Shakespeare as if he is living now and talking to us in our own terms, the 'Shakespeare in blue jeans' approach, you lose that sense of historic distance. But if your approach is too much a historical one, or a traditional one, you end up with a kind of museum theatre, very rhetorical, but just based on beautiful sounding words. You have to find a style between the 'historic' Shakespeare and 'Shakespeare in blue jeans'.

The second problem is that nobody can understand or comprehend even one of the masterpieces as a whole. You cannot perform these days the complete *Othello* or the complete *Hamlet*. In Germany, the plays even today run for about five hours, and in Britain, you can, if you're lucky, get away with three; but you always have to decide with these versions on what aspects of the plays you will concentrate.

Jan Kott made a good remark in 'Hamlet Today' that Hamlet is just like a sponge. It can take everything that you want to put into it – the politics, the psychoanalysis and so on – but you do have to decide what is your major interest in performing it, because otherwise the production lacks a focus. It's not possible just to perform as a literary master-piece and speak all the lines. No one actor can show all the sides to Hamlet in the space of three, four or five hours. This is a problem with all classic plays.

Great directors take clear decisions. But they also try, as the philosopher Ernst Bloch once remarked, to burn the candle of the classics from both ends. I think that there are four major Shakespearian directors in the world today: Peter Brook, Peter Zadek, Akira Kurosawa as a film director and Ariane Mnouchkine of Le Théâtre du Soleil. But I realize that the productions of Mnouchkine and Zadek must seem very strange to English observers.

Why did Mnouchkine choose to use an oriental form as a metaphor for her Shakespearian productions? She had decided that she was not interested in fourteenth-century England or in Shakespeare's time. She wanted to respond to Shakespeare's game with times and places, his projections and reflections. She wanted to make Shakespeare less com-fortable and more strange again, and so bring out the fundamental fury, terror, and emotion, which proceed from Shakespeare's dramatic use of 'suddenness'. Suddenly, somebody changes tack and suddenly somebody decides to throw aside his wife, because of a sudden jealousy or something like that; and the whole world turns suddenly into a tragedy or a comedy. That is one reason why Shake-speare is the greatest dramatist, the abrupt changes of direc-tion in his dramaturgy.

It is a strange power, a vital energy burning within these characters, driving them towards catastrophe. We normally live comfortable lives: we see bombs and the starvation in Africa on television. None of us has that kind of experience which immediately connects with the experiences of

Shakespeare's characters. And so we have to build a bridge to that very strange world, which is far more strange than appears at first to middle-class English directors. I do not want to be chauvinist on this point, but because English directors read the plays in their own language, they often do not understand just how extraordinary the events are; and perhaps this is also a fault which derives from lacking, as Brecht said, a historical perspective.

Peter Zadek, on the other hand, does read Shakespeare in the original. He went to London as a Jewish emigrant with his family as a young boy, and became steeped in English culture and theatre, which is still his great love. For him, Alan Ayckbourn is in a way the most important English playwright after Shakespeare and Oscar Wilde! But he has this tremendously realistic imagination. When he discovered *Othello*, he did not want to tell again the story of a nobleman, suddenly gripped by jealousy and all that. He searched for what Peter Brook calls the sub-text.

Who is this Othello, and what did he mean for the Venetian society, which could be the society of our times? We do not have to travel to South Africa to find the answer. He discovered that Othello for Shakespeare is the same character as is now trivialized as *King Kong and the White Woman* or in *Beauty and the Beast*. Othello was the stereotype of a 'nigger'. Of course, Laurence Olivier wanted to bring out the black in Othello; and he has described how he learnt to walk like an ape and so on. But that is still a formal, technical approach. Zadek wanted to find out how realistically we could present the strange hero. And he decided to present him as seen through the eyes of the Venetian society, and may be our own, as the naive and lascivious 'nigger'.

I won't give you the technical details of his production. It is enough just to tell the story. They go from Venice – or London? – to Cyprus, a nice Mediterranean island, and how do they behave? How do the girls behave, while the men, dressed as British or European colonialist officers with tropical hats and swords, are away, indulging in colonial politics? Desdemona goes to the beach, wearing a bikini, and she spends her time with the wife of another man, in the coffee house and in the tavern, as they would do in the Mediterranean. And there was this nigger . . . . Of course, in the German production we had no nigger, it was a German actor painted black, and when he murdered Desdemona, it was a crime of passion, simply that. It was a clear tragedy, very simple. Shakespeare is sometimes very simple. He had to be. He worked just with actors and with no elaborate stage machinery; and he had to create a world out of their bodies, and he used a simple trick, this black colour. And when he murdered Desdemona and wrestled with her, some of the black colour came off on the white skin of his naked wife, until at the end of the play, he became half-white and half-black. In that way, he became a contemporary. That's why, in my opinion, it was a real Shakespeare production.

'But', asked Kenneth Richards, 'is a production like that interpreting Shakespeare or is it doing something quite different, though equally valid perhaps, using Shakespeare's play as a springboard for a directorial investigation? Would it stand in the same relationship to Shakespeare's *Othello* as Shakespeare's play stands towards his source in Cinthio's *Hecatommithi*?'

Richards then turned to the Greek director, Stavros Doufexis, whose stage productions are much better known in Europe, particularly West Germany, Sweden, and Norway, than they are in Britain. His command of English, for which he always, as here, apologizes, is a constant source of pleasure to those who know him. Startling ideas and images emerge, heightened by the unlikely syntax and the unusual words.

STAVROS DOUFEXIS: If you had asked me some years ago, when I was a small child, if Shakespeare was too English, I would have answered that 'Shakespeare is English', because he wrote beautiful stories with wonderful pictures and he was like an uncle from somewhere. He was not important for me. Uncle Shakespeare lived in another country.

I don't think that I can understand these days what is meant by another country; and I do not really know whether it is important that he was English. Perhaps we should learn to see what is specifically English about Shakespeare, because I have always known Shakespeare from the outside as a foreigner. It is a heavy genius who can come back to England after travelling in a kind of boomerang movement around the whole world. He is a phenomenon, and as a phenomenon, he is always our contemporary and lives in no particular place.

I could ask the same question about the classical Greek writers. Are the Greeks Greek? I suppose that they have a specific meaning for those of us who were born in Greece, than for you who were not; but this is a specific specificity, if I can say that. When I went back to my country after many years, I thought I would like to produce a tragedy. I had never produced a tragedy in Greece, only Shakespeare in Germany. And, you know, I found myself in a place that was absolutely not tragic. For me, the USA is a much more tragic place than Greece at this moment, because society in Greece is purely a capitalistic, an entrepreneurs' society, which is dramatic in itself, but not tragic. I may be able to smell something specifically Greek in the Greek tragedies, but it is not the Greece of today. You may have a similar experience with Shakespeare.

Language is the main problem, but language is not just the way we speak, but the way in which we think and the way in which a theatrical poet devises the totality of the dramatic performance. How can that language survive in translation?

It might sound terrible if I say that I prefer a translation which is less grammatical and more theatrical because we can have both accuracy and actability. But we do lose something when we use a language other than English, just as we lose if we play the Greek tragedies in language other than old Greek. As a foreigner from the other side, I hear you speaking this wonderful Shakespearian English, and I think to myself how good it would be if somebody these days could speak old Greek. It is really wonderful – and why is it wonderful? It is because the sound is of a language very co-ordinated within the English mentality, which we from the other side cannot share. The question for us is whether we might not be able to meet this genius from a different direction, for the power of Shakespeare, the big power, is that of a prophet.

'A prophet with a message?' asked Kenneth Richards. 'Have you found any political or religious philosophy in his works?'

'I think he is a round and full personality', said Doufexis, 'who contains many philosophies. We can, of course, analyse them more closely, which is possibly something that others may do better than the English. Brecht has shown us one way of doing so and many important productions in Germany have been based on his analytical mode.'

Richards then turned to Dr Anna Földes, the author and theatre critic from Hungary.

ANNA FÖLDES: I would like to put this question another way. Is Shakespeare really Hungarian?

There is a typical Hungarian story, about the very well-known Hungarian theatre director, Arthur Bardos, who left Hungary in 1949 to direct *Hamlet* in England; and he was asked by the BBC what it was like to do so. Mr Bardos answered: 'Of course, it is a great honour and a challenge, but to tell you the truth, it's strange to hear the text in English because I am used to the original version, translated by Janos Arany.'

I am not sure whether the name of this classical nineteenth-century poet, Janos Arany, means anything to you, but he was a superlative master and artist in the Hungarian language, who didn't write any plays himself but created his own theatre in translating Shakespeare. He wasn't alone. Many of his colleagues and contemporaries learnt English as he did, to translate Shakespeare.

But the first chapter of the history of Shakespeare in Hungary was written not by poets, but by actors. One of our greatest actors in the late eighteenth century, Gabor Egressy, whom we call the Hungarian Garrick, commissioned and paid for Shakespearian translations so that he could play Richard III, Hamlet, and King Lear. The poets may have had a less personal interest, but they had the need and challenge to provide a complete Hungarian Shakespeare.

Even modern translations go back to these classical nineteenth-century texts. They correct the mistakes and misunderstandings, of course, but contemporary translators have tried to preserve the very well-known words and lines. For a Hungarian, the phrase, 'To be or not to be . . .' means nothing, but 'Lenni vagy nem lenni' is something that you can't forget. It is part of your everyday language.

The Shakespeare cult from the end of the eighteenth century onwards was a phenomenon throughout the whole of Eastern and Central Europe. Shakespeare was the means through which a national self-discovery took place, a way of finding national self-identity. To translate and perform Shakespeare, not from German and not using the German texts but from English, was a common ambition of those patriots who wanted Hungary to find its rightful independence in Europe. The plays were part of a general examination to renew the national language and national acting. After the Hungarian revolution of 1848, during the last decades of despotism, Shakespeare's work preserved the idea of a national independence, freedom and identity.

This attachment to Shakespeare continues today. There are poems about Hamlet which tell us that the Danish prince was not only English but Hungarian; and there is a contemporary play, titled *Hamlet Was Wrong*, written by Margit Gaspar, which was one of the first to criticize the social structure in Hungary during the 1950s, and the cult of the personality, and Stalinism. And there is another by the very talented young author, Geza Beremenyi, called *Halmi*, where you can feel the word 'Hamlet'. It is a kind of paraphrase about the generation gap, about the members of the 1970s generation, who do not feel obliged to correct the sins and crimes of their parents, Claudius or Old Hamlet, and not to interfere with the course of history. It is a discussion with Hamlet.

In 1924, the *Illustrated London News* published an article about Hungarian theatre by the English critic and director, J.T. Grein, who wrote that he had heard more about Shakespeare in one week in Hungary than he had done in a year in England. 'What heights could we have reached,' he speculated, 'if we had had someone in London like Sandor Hevesi?' Sandor Hevesi was a Hungarian national director, who published some books on Shakespeare in Hungary and at that time he was being criticized in Budapest for exaggerating the Shakespeare cult, and Hungarian playwrights were jealous that so much stage time was being occupied by Shakespeare and not by their original works.

In the dark and hopeless days of fascism, young left-wing

theatre people opened up a new chamber theatre in Budapest, and performed *Hamlet*. It was not just a performance but a theatre manifesto. Everybody knew where this Denmark was and what was rotten in it. During the Stalinist period, Shakespeare once more preserved human values in desperate times. It was 1955. I was present as a student on the first night of *Richard III* and I can remember the scene where the scrivener announced the tragic death of Hastings, to fantastic and unusual applause. The sentence without trial, a public murder through accusation and without any real investigation, and without a crime having been committed, had a special political message for those times, when the Rajk trial was still in our minds and not openly discussed.

After Peter Brook's first visit to Hungary, we found out that our way of acting Shakespeare lagged far behind the times. There was a heated discussion about how to play Shakespeare after Brook. The discussion was interesting, but the results were rather dull. In the last decade, we have had a few perfect or, to put it more modestly, up-to-date Shakespearian productions, but also far too many second-rate, conservative interpretations; and in the last few years, we have seen some Shakespeare comedies transformed to suit the tastes of our boulevard theatre.

And so our relationship with Shakespeare is not without its conflicts and problems, but he is still the most familiar, domestic author in our theatre, and has been so for two hundred years. He is the first on the list of foreign authors whose complete works have been translated and published in Hungary; and if you look at the new theatre programme for Budapest, you will see that even today Shakespeare is always and everywhere being performed. I think that we play more Shakespeare in Hungary than you do in England. He's always a box-office success, though not necessarily a real success, an artistic one.

That's why I ask: is he too Hungarian?

At this point, with so much still to discuss, Kenneth Richards reluctantly brought the session to a close. There was a special reason. The IATC had invited Peter Brook to donate a plaque to Jan Kott in recognition of his services to criticism; and this small tribute was about to be paid in the main theatre.

Critics as a rule hate all ceremonials, particularly those which may involve (unlike this one) wearing a tie. On this occasion, however, we felt that a reunion between two men who between them had transformed productions of Shakespeare's plays needed to be especially witnessed; and so we invited the audiences in the studio to join those in the main theatre, who had been discussing Shakespearian verse-speaking. It turned out to be an unexpectedly moving occasion, with more reunions taking place (as between past and present, East and West, Marxists and capitalists) than we had jotted down in our agendas.

TO JAN KOTT

At midday, on Sunday, 19 October 1986, Peter Brook presented, on behalf of the International Association of Theatre Critics, a plaque to Jan Kott, in recognition of his services to criticism.

PETER BROOK: Ever since I started working in the theatre, I have been struck by one extraordinary fact, that the only thing that matters is what is happening at the moment when it is happening.

Jan Kott has just reminded me that, twenty-six years ago, we met under lurid and melodramatic circumstances at night in Warsaw; and as we walked from one police station to another, to fill in the long, boring streets, we started talking about Shakespeare, and immediately found that the one thing that could provoke an exchange, the one point where a common understanding could arise, was this shared sense of how the timeless and what's happening now come together.

Being contemporary does not necessarily mean blindly bringing everything down to the present, nor does being timeless mean just being in a dream, so loftily elevated that the present has no importance. There is a point at which the great myths of the past and our sensation of living in the present, here and now, come together. This fusion is what I have always found so thrilling in all your writings. There is, of course, great erudition, scholarship, and imaginative penetration into the deep movements of history; but these have never lost that link with what can only really concern us, the actual moment we're living now.

When I first heard about this opportunity of coming over to London to have the pleasure of paying this personal homage to my friend, I hadn't actually heard about the theme of these discussions: Is Shakespeare still our contemporary? And then I meet my old friend for the first time in many years – and see the answer. If yesterday, somebody had said to me, 'How is Jan Kott? Is he *contemporary*?' I might have been tempted to develop a theory like this, 'Well, you know, he wrote in a certain period . . . .' But now I suddenly see you, I see the look in the eye, the sharp sense of what is humorous and the exact sense of what is going on, that vitality, and I can say, 'Jan Kott, Contemporary!'

There's a solid piece of present. That's why in English it's called 'a present'.

JAN KOTT: I am greatly moved just to be in London, to be enlightened by this conference, and to meet Peter. It was one of the most important days of my life to see *Titus Andronicus*, with Laurence Olivier, directed by Peter; and the beginning of the beginning of my book was with that production perhaps! After that, my life changed. I was invited by Peter to come to London, which was then a long, long way. I'm not very young, and yet to receive this gift, after twenty-six, twenty-seven years of my book, from this organization! And to be here! I would like to say to all of you – and first of all to my wife, Lidia – my book, as you know, was dedicated to my wife – how happy I am to be here!

DOES SHAKESPEARE'S VERSE
SEND YOU TO SLEEP?

with
Sheila Allen, Alexander Anikst,
Tony Church, David Thacker, and, in
the chair, Michael Billington

Nowadays, when we talk about the musicality of Shakespeare's verse, we are praising sounds other than those he would have heard. John Barton, the Shakespearian scholar and a director of the Royal Shakespeare Company, once tried to reconstruct Elizabethan diction, broadening and deepening the vowel sounds until they sounded a bit Devonish. American scholars likened the results to the English spoken in the Appalachians.

Modern pronunciation flattens and lightens the vowel sounds, leaving a blander sound to the verse and quickening the speed of delivery. Under those circumstances, the metrical stress become a barely conscious hidden beat, blurring verse and prose, and sometimes sounding like a hypnotic throb.

Nor are audiences particularly sensitive to theatrical verse. At one time, and in all oral cultures, verse was an essential aid to memory. If a syllable was lost, the line sounded wrong, and so you could guess that a word was missing, perhaps vital to the sense. Nowadays, we can check the line against a written text, without depending upon what we think we have heard.

Against the background of our predominantly naturalistic theatrical traditions, verse sounds like an unnecessary ornament; and sometimes it conflicts with the natural pauses and hesitations that a modern actor uses to indicate a sub-text. Poor verse-speaking does not necessarily indicate the technical incompetence of the actor. The actor could simply have been trained in a different tradition. The American Method actors, who studied with Lee Strasberg, were well equipped to act in Arthur Miller's plays, but they could stumble blindly through Shakespeare's.

Actors also face, from a different direction, the problem that the translators found so troublesome. Shakespeare uses language connotatively, rather than denotatively; but audiences can become confused if they are expecting one meaning, and one only, from a verse line and are then confronted with several. An actor has to make sure that the primary meaning is clear, together with, if possible, some secondary meanings. This can involve awkward decisions about the text.

In *King Lear*, for example, Goneril has an apparently simple line, 'My fool usurps my body' (IV.ii.28), but the word fool has several Shakespearian meanings. It can mean a court jester or someone who has behaved unwisely. It often refers to sexual infatuation, either the passion itself or the passion's object, like a toy-boy. It can be a term of endearment or an insult.

In this scene, Goneril has just parted from the bastard Edmund, with whom she has fallen in love, and is about to greet her husband, Albany, whom she has come to despise; and so the word fool could refer either to Edmund or Albany – or she could be using the word in a more abstract sense, to mean her personal passion. In the National Theatre production of *King Lear*, then in rehearsal, the director, David Hare, cut through these complications by changing the line to 'A fool usurps my bed', which, at best, says only part of what Shakespeare might have meant. But it was a straightforward line which did not worry the audience or the actress who spoke it, and to that extent, might be considered more theatrically effective.

The author, broadcaster and theatre critic of the *Guardian*, Michael Billington, who was also at that time the chairman of the British section of the IATC, presided over this session, and he began by asking the actor and director Tony Church whether or not we 'pay lip service to Shakespeare's language without acknowledging the difficulties of vocabulary, syntax and meaning that it contains?'

*

TONY CHURCH: I was intrigued at a conference recently when a professor said, 'I think we're guilty sometimes of making Shakespeare too easy.' I took him to task on this, and he said, 'Well, the fact is that he contains in a line so many different possible meanings that we often take a very simplistic view and lose out on the theatrical excitements which we might gain from really mining the contradictions.'

But I was always taught that if you actually examine the verse, not just its content but its form, you find through the use of imagery, rhythm and all the other devices, a highly complex and frequently contradictory view of the motives and the behaviour patterns of the people who are speaking.

The verse contains so many clues to psychology, to action of all kinds, as well as scene-painting and time-painting, that if you really mine it out, and go for all the individual nuggets in it, you've got a huge quantity of little plays going on. I don't see how it can conceivably send anybody to sleep.

If you just blandly trot through and hope, as Peter Brook once said, that the verse will go on by itself, like a railway train on tracks, then it can become boring. The problem is that very often people do just that, they let the train run and don't actually drive it. It's possible to get away with Shakespeare by just letting the train run on its tracks, because the rhythm will go on, the shapes, the melodies will go on; and for years, from when I started going to the theatre, that's how people spoke Shakespeare – and I did go to sleep for parts of it. It washed over me. Nowadays, I hope, we are trying to mine out those different colours and contradictions. It may be difficult, it's certainly hard work, but any acting is hard work in rehearsal, as it should be. If you do that, you have a huge battery of information, probably more than from most dramatists, although you may not have stage directions and prefaces and all the back-up comment that you get from modern writers. What you have instead is an extraordinary code-book for action.

Billington then asked David Thacker whether he agreed that 'if you go for the ambiguities and contradictions in Shakespeare's verse, that will in itself engage an audience?'

DAVID THACKER: I'm not sure that I would approach the problem in quite this way. I remember listening on radio to an extract from Richard Burton's Hamlet – 'What a piece of work is man, how noble in reason, how infinite in faculty . . . the beauty of the world, the paragon of animals' – and I remember thinking, 'That's the way to speak Shakespearian verse!' and, of course, it's in prose.

There's a false distinction between his verse and his prose, because if you look through the canon of his work there's an enormous variety in the forms of his verse. In *The Winter's Tale*, there is the compact, intense imagery of Leontes' lines, when he starts to suspect Hermione, his wife, who is innocently welcoming Polixenes:

> Too hot, too hot!
> To mingle friendship far is mingling bloods.
> I have a *tremor cordis* on me: my heart dances,
> But not for joy, not joy.
>
> (I.ii.109)

That is from one of his later plays, but if you look at *Julius Caesar*, the language is much more simple and straightforward. You don't have to puzzle over the meaning of Cassius's lines:

> Why, man, he doth bestride the narrow world
> Like a Colossus, and we petty men
> Walk under his huge legs, and peep about
> To find ourselves dishonourable graves.
> Men at some time are masters of their fates:
> The fault, dear Brutus, is not in our stars
> But in ourselves, that we are underlings.
>
> (I.ii.133)

The aim in working on the plays, whether the particular passage is in prose or verse, is to get to the heart of the metaphorical life of the language. The actors have to grasp, first of all, the literal sense of what is being said. If an actor has to say 'Who would fardels bear?' he has to know what the word 'fardels' means. But the second stage is to understand the emotional content, the drive, of the scene.

This is where the big change has happened in our attitudes towards verse speaking over the past twenty years. No actor worth his or her salt would be satisfied now by simply trotting through the text in some half-comprehending way. They need to know what is motivating the character, what emotionally is happening, what he or she is talking about. If I say 'To be or not to be, that is the question', am I about to kill myself? Do I literally have my dagger here? Is now the moment to kill myself? Or should I put up with life and all its burdens? If an actor responds to the scene in that immediate way, it becomes an intense emotional experience; and the play becomes a succession of such powerful moments, which can be communicated to the audience, even if the precise detail of what is happening, word for word, is not actually grasped or appreciated.

'And so it's not the verse that sends people to sleep', said Michael Billington, 'but unfelt, unthought-through renderings of it, which modern actors avoid. I'm glad to hear it. But at Stratford, I have seen people asleep, haven't you, Sheila Allen?'

'Yes', said the actress Sheila Allen, 'and I've sometimes gone to sleep myself, I'm ashamed to say. You've had a tiring day, you're in the warm and you drop off!'

SHEILA ALLEN: One of the problems is that Shakespeare can be ruined for us at school. We're told that we've got to do Shakespeare. Some of us can get intrigued early on, some instinctively pick up the music, but he is not taught as a living writer. We're presented with these scripts of four hundred years ago – and they're in a language which 'apparently' isn't modern and in a form that isn't 'apparently' like modern speech – and we get confused, and draw back. And unless we're very fortunate to have an enlightened first guide to Shakespeare's works, or second guide, that is how we remain, stuck there, in a panic!

In 1966, I had the luck to be invited to take on a three-year contract with the Royal Shakespeare Company at Stratford. I was also pregnant, and I played the part of Lady Percy in *Henry IV, Parts One* and *Two*. And every matinée, I had to have a solo sonnet session with John Barton. These sessions were a revelation for me. I am delighted that John Barton has become world-famous for his TV series and the book on Shakespearian verse-speaking, which was based on the transcripts. Like so many theatre people, I had come across the Method in between leaving drama school in 1951 and becoming a professional actor; and many actors trained in the Method have problems when they come into contact with Shakespeare. But after working with John Barton, I became convinced that there was no contradiction between the Method approach and Shakespearian acting.

He told me three things. 'Sheila, will you' – now please take this with a pinch of salt, for it is an instruction given to an actress in an acting workshop – 'will you make a tiny pause at the end of each Shakespearian line.' 'Sheila, will you please stop using your Method pause in the middle of a Shakespearian line to express a thought which has just occurred to you.' And, 'Sheila, you will notice that in every Shakespearian verse line, towards the end, the last word, there is a very evocative image for the speaker – and then notice how, within the first three words of the following line, there is an even stronger image.' I am not talking about the entire play, but about the particular speaker, the character, and how the verse knits together. And it was not a lesson which could be learnt quickly. I had a lot of time to absorb it, for the productions of *Henry IV* ran for six months, and being pregnant, I may have been in a more receptive mood. Anyway, this approach fascinated me.

Time passed. In 1973, I was invited to play, oh dear, the Scottish lady, with another theatre company. I am not one of those fortunate people who instinctively know where the line ending is. I can't count. I have to learn. When we were rehearsing with the text, I thought, 'John's right! Isn't that amazing?'

But that was when I had the text still in front of me. When we did the first run-through without the text, it was a different matter. It was a Saturday morning. I thought I was doing all the same things that I had done in rehearsal, the same intention, the same thoughts, the same reactions and interaction with the other actors. But I felt I was on a skid-pan, you know? when a car hits an oil slick. Except I was the one who was skidding. The director wasn't worried but I went home in a hell of a depression. I thought, 'I know what it is. I don't know my line endings.'

And so I sat down in my chair, I picked up the book and started from the beginning again. Well, Lady Macbeth actually begins speaking in prose – and prose is equally fascinating but it doesn't pose the same problems as verse – and I became involved in the problems of that opening scene. Why does Shakespeare give Lady Macbeth a nine minute solo? She's the leading lady, but still, *nine minutes*! The messenger has just come in to give her Macbeth's letter, which she reads, but why does she talk for so long about the possibilities? And in verse?

She reads the prose letter, 'They met me in the day of success, and I have learned by the perfect'st report they have more in them than mortal knowledge.' And so on. But when she starts to think about what her husband has written, she turns to verse.

> Glamis thou art, and Cawdor, and shalt be
> What thou art promised.
>
> (I.v.13)

The verse line ends after 'be'. That was what was going wrong in rehearsal. I forgot where the end of the line came, and I started to think about the first three or four words of the next line, 'What thou art promised.' Why does Shakespeare use a euphemism to describe what he's already put down in black and white in the letter? 'King that shalt be.' That one little thing, the pause after 'be' and the revealing euphemism that follows, helped me to make sense of the rest of the scene.

'That is a very good example', said Michael Billington, 'of the usefulness of following rules. It makes the sense clearer. But what happens in other countries where these rules do not apply?' He turned to Alexander Anikst.

ALEXANDER ANIKST: Before we decide how to speak Shakespeare, we have to consider the nature of Shakespeare's theatre. In Russia, we have a very strong realistic tradition in the theatre, and so when Russian actors play Shakespeare, they try to give you the psychology of the person. You probably all know Stanislavski's plan for staging *Othello*. He wrote an imaginary biography for Othello, trying to explain every speech, every movement.

Personally, I don't believe that Shakespeare is very realistic in this way. I share the opinion of those scholars who regard Shakespeare's theatre as a kind of transition from medieval theatre to modern theatre. It owes a great deal to the morality tradition, but it is already partly concerned with individual psychologies, partly but not completely. And you have to make up your mind about this point before you can decide how to speak Shakespeare.

Take, for example, the dagger speech in *Macbeth*. It can be spoken as a kind of confession, as you might speak Claudius's prayer in *Hamlet*. For the modern theatre-goer, Macbeth can sound as if he is confessing his sins. But I do not think that such speeches are psychological. They are philosophical, ethical, what you like, but they are Shakespeare's way of telling his audience that this man is wrong. Macbeth is accusing his own actions – as does Claudius. But in real life, criminals would probably try to justify themselves, to find some excuse that would make them less wicked. Shakespeare is going against psychology, and this is the real problem nowadays, how to deliver such speeches.

DAVID THACKER: There is another clear example in *Hamlet* at the end of the nunnery scene. Hamlet goes off, having abused Ophelia. In some productions, he hits her, he throws her about – and in others, it's just verbal abuse; but Ophelia is usually left in a heap on the floor. Realistically, Polonius and the King should come in immediately to comfort her, and there's no reason why they shouldn't, except that Ophelia has a soliloquy! She must be in a totally shattered state of mind, but look what language she uses!

> O, what a noble mind is here o'erthrown!
> The courtier's, soldier's, scholar's, eye, tongue, sword,
> Th'expectancy and rose of the fair state,
> The glass of fashion and the mould of form,
> Th'observ'd of all observers, quite, quite down!

then, at the very end of the speech, comes the line which psychologically you might expect,

> O woe is me,
> T'have seen what I have seen, see what I see.
> (III.i.152)

Ophelia should be *in extremis*, but, as if she is speaking in a time warp, she delivers one of the most formal, balanced, delicately weighed out, almost as if in a jeweller's scales, pieces of verse!

The only way in which Ophelia can hang on to her reason is by making a formal construction from what has happened. She is hanging on to her sanity by her fingernails and in moments like that, we have to be precise and careful for the only alternative otherwise is to scream. Shakespeare has thrown down a huge challenge which every Ophelia has to face. In a moment of intense emotional crisis, she has to speak a perfectly balanced, carefully constructed poem.

Sheila Allen and David Thacker both wanted to comment on what Alexander Anikst had said about *Macbeth* and whether the dagger speech was naturalistic.

SHEILA ALLEN: Would Macbeth have talked about his wrongdoing like that? I think he would. He knows he's wrong and the dramatic excitement is this, will he continue? I never see that play without wanting him to win. Shakespeare does bring out this ambiguity. It's not easy to take sides, especially not in the history plays. The Shakespeare plays I like to watch are those where I'm not sure of whose side I'm on!

DAVID THACKER: I'm in Stanislavski's camp. Clearly the language isn't naturalistic. It is loaded with images and for much of the time in verse; but the same basic principles apply for an actor. He or she needs to know, 'What am I talking about? What am I doing – and why?' But for that reason, I'd also like to slug it out with John Barton, for what Sheila Allen has described is, I believe, exactly the wrong way of tackling Shakespearian verse.

I cannot believe that the playwright sat around deciding that the last word in an iambic pentameter has to have this special significance. The examination of the text suggests that you need to get the clearest, most literal meaning of the words, which may span half a dozen lines, perhaps more. And I would call as my star witness Hamlet, who instructed the players to 'suit the action to the word, the word to the action with this special observance . . . to hold, as t'were, the mirror up to nature'. It's clear to me that he is asking his actors to provide a clear and comprehensive imitation of humanity, whereas Alexander Anikst's view, if I have understood it correctly, is that we're not talking about psychological realism in that way.

ALEXANDER ANIKST: *Hamlet* is very interesting from the point of view of theatre history. In it, there are three distinct styles of play. There is, first of all, the actors' performance of *The Murder of Gonzago*, which they play as they had done in the past, from the days long before Shakespeare, at the end of the Middle Ages and at the start of Elizabethan theatre. But then there is the play from which Priam's monologue comes, and it is in a different style. And so you have two styles of dramatic action and two types of verse. You will remember that the Gonzago play is in rhymed couplets and Priam's monologue is in blank verse.

But then there is the third play, the one which we are watching, the tragedy written by Shakespeare. And that is in yet another style, which we are made to feel is like life, because the two other styles have been so artificial. When you speak about Shakespeare's style, and what he wants from the theatre, you have to bear in mind that he brought the problems of the theatre before his time into *Hamlet*.

'Traditionally', Michael Billington said, 'the advice to the players has always been taken rather reverently, as Shakespeare's last word on Theatre. Nowadays, there's a tendency to treat it much more cynically, as if Hamlet has had the puppyish arrogance to tell professional actors how to do their job. Well, is it a bit of cheek, or isn't it?'

TONY CHURCH: It's also a bit of cheek for directors to assume that it is a bit of cheek. It's quite possible to retain the ambiguity – to have a Hamlet who is perhaps being cheeky, but at the same time deadly serious, extremely concerned and almost with the suggestion that it is Shakespeare's concern, and for a leading actor to treat the advice as if he were being patronized. You can have both meanings, but it's naughty to load the speech with this fashionable idea that Hamlet is just a badly behaved boy. It is fashionable nowadays to present Claudius as the new hero of *Hamlet*. Well, he may be a sympathetic character, but he's not the hero.

But I am fascinated by Alexander Anikst's point that the play contains three styles – medieval morality play, Marlowe, and Shakespeare, if you want to put it like that.

DAVID THACKER: And it's also interesting how Hamlet describes the actor who speaks the Priam speech. The speech itself may be too long. Well, it's too long for Polonius. But Hamlet says,

> Is it not monstrous that this player here,
> But in a fiction, in a dream of passion,
> Could force his soul so to his own conceit
> That from her working all his visage wann'd,
> Tears in his eyes, distraction in's aspect,
> A broken voice, and his whole function suiting
> With forms to his conceit? And all for nothing.
>
> (II.ii.545)

The problem with doing *Hamlet* is that you need your best actor to play the First Player. Hamlet has got to be intensely moved and very impressed!

TONY CHURCH: The contradiction is wonderful, for Shakespeare deliberately takes a rather contrived and old-fashioned speech and makes it clear that the actor has broken through that into realism. You have to play every technical device in that speech brilliantly – and also provide the image of a psychological breakdown.

DAVID THACKER: Acting Shakespeare is incredibly hard. You need a combination of technical facility and emotional control, to be able to understand and give expression to the sense and nature of the language. And he also requires a deep understanding of your own experiences.

But I would still need a lot of convincing that the last word in a verse line has a special significance!

SHEILA ALLEN: Can I clarify that point? I was talking about a study technique, because if you look at the line, and the feelings within it, and how they are expressed through the details of the verse structure, then you find it easier to discover the emotions and their relative weights.

If you look at the whole speech or section, all you get is generalization.

DAVID THACKER: What Shakespeare requires an actor to do is, if they've done the preparation, to throw caution to the winds. If you're playing Claudius and say, 'Oh, my offence is rank!', you must have an imaginative sense of the rank nature of your offence, its smell.

ALEXANDER ANIKST: I still insist that in my country, actors have great difficulty in speaking Shakespeare because they have been brought up on modern, realistic writings. For actors who come from this tradition, the reading of blank verse is difficult. And it is similar in England. What you call psychology is not psychology at all, it's romantic emotion. You can reach the spectator by reciting fierily. Be fiery with emotion and you will move people. But that is not psychology. That is emotion.

There are three levels of verse speaking in *Hamlet*, the primitive, the emotional and romantic (Priam's speech), and the Shakespearian intellectual style of the play itself. The way in which Hamlet speaks is sometimes emotionally romantic and sometimes philosophically analytical. And so we cannot talk about a single style when we speak of Shakespeare.

A member of the audience returned to Ophelia's speech, quoted by Thacker, and said that it may be poetry but it is also a male view as to how a woman might react. It was simply too formal an expression of her feelings; and this was what Harriet Walter found so difficult in the Royal Court production, after she had been assaulted by Jonathan Pryce's Hamlet.

'That is a problem', conceded Thacker, 'but Shakespeare deliberately wrote it like that because the scene is at such a pitch.' ' Yes', agreed Church, 'the emotions of the moment hit against the form. It's like a lid on a pressure cooker. That's what makes it exciting.'

'Isn't the real problem', asked Michael Billington, 'not Shakespeare's lack of understanding of the female psychology, but the extremism of the production? Every production these days seems to up the stakes! It's got wilder and wilder in that scene, with Hamlet dragging her around by the hair and pommelling her about. And then she's got to stand up and deliver that soliloquy. Of course, it's a problem for an actress, but that's not Shakespeare's fault.'

'You've got to ask the question', said Tony Church, 'what is Hamlet trying to achieve in that scene? I think that an examination of the text reveals that he's trying to achieve two things. One is to tell Ophelia that, whatever happens, she mustn't stay in a corrupt society where women are like his mother, marrying again moments after their husbands have died, and the second is to convince those who are listening that he's really mad . . . .'

'But does he *know* they're listening?' asked Thacker. 'I'm sorry. That's interpretation!'

110

A member of the audience objected to both these motives. 'One of the interesting things about this scene is that Hamlet is confused. He wants to save Ophelia. He wants to send her to a nunnery – but at the same time, he does accuse her of being a whore, which is how he sees his mother. All women have become frail, all women have become whores. And so he's torn apart, not knowing whether to save her or abuse her. That's the attitude he also has to himself, sometimes lashing himself, sometimes wanting to protect himself through the disguise of madness. When Derek Jacobi played that scene, it was tremendous. When he said, "I'll no more on't, it hath made me mad!", you suddenly realized that he was just as much a victim as Ophelia, though he was playing her persecutor.'

'I'd like to remind the panel of the title of this session', intervened a member of the audience. 'It's all been very entertaining, but I'd like to know why, bearing in mind all the exciting, thrilling stuff you've been talking about, nine out of ten productions of Shakespeare I see are dreadfully boring? Is the theory more interesting than the practice? Shakespeare can't survive on intellectual snobbery. He's got to win new audiences all the time.'

'And so we do', said Sheila Allen. 'But you've admitted yourself', said Tony Church, 'that you do fall asleep during some productions.'

'When I fall asleep', retorted Sheila Allen, 'it's usually because the actors are doing their psychological, emotional realism, whatever you want to call it, and are ruining the language. The man writes with such precision that the psyche is linked with his guts, and he has to put it all down black and white on the page. We simply have to find out, four hundred years later, how to do it. When I fall asleep, it's because the actors have not grasped the pot of gold that's been handed to them. They're either over-colouring the scene or not using the dexterity of the language.'

'At Stratford', added Billington, 'they seem to be desperate at this moment to find different ways of doing Shakespeare, to make him more relevant! There's a heavy scenic element. We're over-decorating and over-dressing Shakespeare and not engaging with the texts, as we used to. But I don't usually find these productions boring in the sense of being dull or not thought through.'

'For my taste', said a member of the audience, 'I feel that the more you try to get the audience to empathize with the characters, to make them more recognizable by reducing the language, the less effect you have. I am sure that Shakespeare wanted to impress his audiences with the voluptuousness of the language and its variety. There are passages in Shakespeare which you should really let wash over you, just as there are passages where you should bring it down into close-up, into naturalistic or nearly naturalistic drama.'

TONY CHURCH: We always tend to talk as if there's one

approach to playing Shakespeare, whereas, of course, there are many different methods. You can't approach *Romeo and Juliet*, a play of extreme lyrical intensity, whose voluptuous feel extends far beyond its psychological interest, as you would do *The Winter's Tale*, which is jagged, rich with psychological insight.

In 1964, Peter Brook was at a conference on translating Shakespeare in Prague and he was asked, 'What is the right style for translating Shakespeare?' And he stood up and said, 'There is no one style for translating Shakespeare, or a scene by Shakespeare, and there are even places where the style must change within the line!' And he sat down.

Several members of the audience wanted to explain why Shakespeare sometimes sent them to sleep. One said, 'I find Shakespeare under instant translation in my mind for much of the time. I go to his plays partly for the intellectual effort of trying to understand all the wonderful things that are being said. I'm not actually *bored*, but I do know that I can't cope with it!' 'Some productions', said another, 'become boring because they seem so narcissistic. This is particularly true of the subsidized companies. They've become so stylized that they've lost the need to communicate with the audience.'

'In the classroom', added a third, 'when we first learn about Shakespeare, you're not usually allowed to enjoy the emotional openness of the characters, and how they're reacting to the situation. Let's take a simple example. In *Romeo and Juliet*, there is a line, "Oh, she doth teach the torches to burn bright!" A young man has just seen a very beautiful girl and he searches around for ways of describing his feelings. That's the psychological reality and it also paints for the audience the emotional completeness and fullness of the moment. The difficulty with Shakespeare, and the reason why his plays can send you to sleep, is (a) we don't surrender to that immediate moment and (b) the actor has to be completely open. There is no holding back. We live in the twentieth century where we don't go around, saying about our girl friends, "My God, she teaches the torches to burn bright!" or something like that. We hold back. But we have got to believe, in order to feel the Shakespearian moment, that *this* character at *this* moment would have chosen that phrase as the most perfect expression of how he feels.'

'I'd like to turn this title around', said another speaker, 'and construe it as a compliment. What it could mean is that you're hearing someone on stage saying something so lyrical that you're only concerned with listening to its rhythm and pattern. I find the same thing with Irish drama. I switch off listening to the meaning. I just tune in to the music coming from the stage. There are passages which are meant just to wash over you, as has been said, and the experience, indeed the gist of its meaning, lies in the rhythm, not in word-by-word analysis.'

'Still', said Michael Billington, 'it can't help if it sends you to sleep. My belief is that it's not Shakespeare's verse that sends you to sleep, but those horrendous package tours where you do Oxford in the afternoon and Stratford in the evening. You should come to a Shakespeare play, or any play for that matter, intellectually fresh.'

The last speaker from the audience attempted to reconcile the different opinions between Sheila Allen and David Thacker about the importance of the verse form. 'I don't think it's a conflict at all', he started bravely, 'Thacker emphasized the content, and Sheila Allen the form. But we must have *both* content *and* form! The form expresses the content! You can't have one without the other. And unless you have *both*, you have a sure recipe for sending the audience to sleep!'

'You seldom do get both though', said Thacker gloomily. 'It's very difficult.'

DOES SHAKESPEARE WRITE BETTER FOR TELEVISION?

with
Elijah Moshinsky and, in the chair,
John Elsom

When the Chorus asks in *Henry V*,

> Can this cockpit hold
> The vasty fields of France? Or may we cram
> Within this wooden O the very casques
> That did affront the air at Agincourt?
>
> (Prologue: 11)

he expects the answer 'No', and he apologizes to everyone for daring to try. But on television, he could have shown those fields (or those of Vietnam), without having to call upon 'a Muse of fire' to make up for the defects in his technology.

We can, of course, consider whether a photograph of a killing field is more or less of a 'cipher' than Shakespeare's verbal description of it. Neither the image nor the word is identical with Agincourt; but film can provide quick, precise pictures of places and situations which Shakespeare has to summon to our minds by what might be regarded as the more cumbersome means of language. But are words more cumbersome or do they just focus the mind in a different way?

In this discussion, we wanted to consider television versions of Shakespeare and two much broader questions. Would Shakespeare have found his task easier if he had been able to use the resources of film, television and modern stage technology? And does our familiarity with the visual imagery of the new media mean that Shakespeare's stagecraft seems to us primitive and therefore a barrier to our appreciation?

The main speaker was Elijah Moshinsky, the British director, whose television productions of *Coriolanus* and *All's Well That Ends Well* for the BBC had been singled out for critical praise, although the BBC's attempt

114

to offer the complete cycle of Shakespeare's plays had generally received indifferent reviews. I began by asking Moshinsky his opinion of the BBC Shakespeares.

ELIJAH MOSHINSKY: If I start to talk about that series, from an artistic point of view, and the whole matter of Shakespeare on television, I'm opening an enormous can of worms.

The whole canon has now been done for the BBC, and sold to America, and packaged for schools; and it is unlikely that we're going to see any similar Shakespearian projects for eight or nine years. The commercial channels will not find the money to do it; and the BBC certainly won't want to compete with their own product. This discussion really should have taken place before some of the more awful mistakes were made.

Before considering the artistic problems, I want to describe some of the practical ones. We had five or six days in the studio to make one of those BBC Shakespeares. It was decreed early on that none should be shot on location. There was a *Henry VIII* that used outside broadcasting techniques on location, but that was ten years ago when the lightweight video techniques, the one inch tape that we now use, didn't exist. Nor did the current editing techniques exist. It is only in the past six years that we've been able to edit video tapes with the precision of film. And so when the series started, you had to have lots of cameras and technical back-up crews, and it was all too difficult and expensive to go on location, or to use mixed location and studio. And so, finally, we had to make these plays in the studio in five or six days, with no overrun. I never actually did finish *A Midsummer Night's Dream*. Some people thought that it was just a daring, and outrageous, piece of text cutting, but actually I just didn't get around to the end, because at ten o'clock, they pulled the plugs.

We were allowed four weeks' rehearsal before that with a group of actors who were not part of a company, but assembled for that particular production. Within those four weeks, you had to find a viable way, technically, of doing the Shakespeare play as well as getting the actors to perform it. On top of that, it was deemed important by the *Time-*

Life people who co-produced the series with the BBC that there should be none of this modern business of updating. It either had to be set in Shakespeare's time or in the little period that tradition has assigned to the play. In the case of *A Midsummer Night's Dream*, that's either 1590 or ancient Greece. They felt very strongly about that because they thought that otherwise they couldn't sell the product to schools in America, or other institutions. The actual Shakespeare series has made a lot of money for the BBC. It's proved to be an enormous amount, because the series has a very long after-life and American schools love it. It's still being bought, particularly the rarer plays, *All's Well, Timon of Athens*, that sort of play . . .

Within that structure, there was the matter of artistic freedom. I was brought in quite late, when Jonathan Miller became the producer – and suddenly the whole project had opened up and we were allowed to take artistic decisions. Until then, it was more like Hollywood and no artistic decisions were made. It was meant to be a traditional product, marketed for schools. I have to mention this, because our very discussion today about Shakespeare on television really hasn't happened before. Nobody discussed it properly. But one interesting thing did happen.

When the first of the series went out, *Romeo and Juliet*, it was so poor that it was almost a laughing stock. But by the time we had finished, attitudes had changed. A very interesting reversal had occurred in performing styles, which is worth mentioning. When we started, the Royal Shakespeare Company was performing in a way that was considered almost cinematically modern, in terms of speech and delivery. By the time we had finished the series, we had discovered how to perform the text cinematically in an intimate fashion, while in contrast the RSC had suddenly become Victorian in its production style.

And that is really the crucial question, for if there's anything useful to be gained from performing Shakespeare on television (as distinct from the big screen), it is this ability to be able to speak those lines, whisper them, use them as voice-overs, anything except having to think about how to project them and pump them full of too much energy. The RSC meanwhile had moved to the Barbican and they had developed a bombastic style of delivery, which was rather two-dimensional. As we were evolving this television style, we discovered that the characters had to become more dense in their psychology. The production of the voice and the speaking had to be extraordinarily subtle to succeed, because basically you are always working in close-up, in a space more intimate than this studio.

In my view, enormous consequences developed from playing *All's Well That Ends Well* on television, because suddenly it became a very intimate play. I think that the RSC's production of *All's Well* with Peggy Ashcroft, which was hailed as being so Chekhovian, was actually heralded by our television version, which was, if anything, more intimate and mood-laden. There is also much to be gained by the actors who had to enter into the lives of the characters even more closely and realistically, in order to speak their thoughts. They couldn't deliver the lines like stage actors; and that was the particular discipline that television imposed upon Shakespearian speech.

From my point of view as a director, there were three areas, apart from the enormous technical problems, which I found artistically challenging. One was the setting. Cardboard sets in studios are continual threats to Shakespeare on television, because the audience is watching a screen, not a space. All modern dramaturgy is concerned with the actor in space; and suddenly I found that all our modern theories about staging, from Tyrone Guthrie onwards, my whole theoretical framework, was irrelevant.

It was very strange, working without theoretical support. Were we looking at an actor in space? Should we imagine Rome or somewhere? I once discussed this matter with Jane Howell who was doing the history plays, and she argued that the way out of this problem was to present the play so that the audience could see a studio. They could sense the space within which you were working as the camera moved around the studio. My solution kept changing, and sometimes it worked and sometimes it didn't, but I thought that the result should be more like a picture, a photograph or a painting. You had to deal with the two-dimensional

117

aspect of the medium. My approach had considerable drawbacks. I got into this difficulty which I couldn't solve. To make Shakespeare's stagecraft work for the flat screen and the two-dimensional picture, I found myself cutting out entrances and exits, so that the movement became terribly static. But an actor making an entrance seemed very false and theatrical, because the eye had become accustomed to looking at a two-dimensional image.

If you cut out exits and entrances and had everyone just sitting in chairs, with the camera discovering them, then you had to make intuitive guesses as to where you were. What was the reality being presented to you? Were you in a studio? Were you in Rome? Or were you in a picture of Rome, or a picture of Illyria, or wherever?

What emerged from the television Shakespeares, what became the most dynamic element, was the use of the actors' faces: not the whole body, but the face. Different actors succeeded in different ways, but when I did *All's Well* with Celia Johnson, it was her face that told you the story of the Countess as much as her performance. And you started to cast plays from actors' portraits and what they could tell you.

The other real problem is that you don't know the kind of circumstances in which a television Shakespeare is being viewed. You have no control at all over the audience. When you direct on a stage, you assemble your ideas of the play, your reading of it, and you work with the actors, who perform it; and they have some control over the audience. They can make an audience want to watch and listen, or not, by their presence and skill. But on television they have no such control. There is even less control on television than in a film, because the audience has not made the voluntary effort to come to a darkened room to see it.

A director has no control over the scale of the picture. Somebody could be watching it on a three inch black-and-white set or on a twenty inch monitor. The colour on my set could be different from the colour on yours. I was in Japan once and saw one of my programmes dubbed into Japanese and broken into quarter-of-an-hour segments to put in the advertisements. It was *A Midsummer Night's*

Dream. And they'd cut out all the bits they thought were boring, without leaving any sense of continuity at all. It was all very weird because the result bore no relationship to how I thought the programme should go out.

That was also my problem when *A Midsummer Night's Dream* first went out at Christmas time, some five or six years ago. In between Parts One and Two, there was the News – and on this occasion the news was that the Russian troops had moved into Poland. And so you had the first part of *The Dream*, then the Russians moved into Poland, and then the second festive part of *The Dream*. That's Shakespeare on television. These are problems quite apart from the theoretical matters that you might want to discuss. The medium is not one where you can just put a play on the screen but expect it to be watched as a play. The play is being scattered abroad in a most curious fashion.

'I'm surprised you described television acting as a discipline', said a member of the audience, 'because I would have thought that it would have been an even harder discipline to reach the audience at the back of the stalls in the Barbican. Of course, Shakespeare can be very rhetorical, but I would have thought that the more intimate medium of television is, in a way, more natural for the actor, even though the camera and the lights are glaring at you. But I'm not an actor.'

'Is there an actor in the house?' I asked, and one replied, 'Yes, I've had some experience on television and yes, I do think it's an extremely difficult discipline. There are quite as many pressures equal in effect if not in type to those in a proscenium arch or in-the-round theatre. Of course, when you're performing to a live audience, there are the pressures we all know about, and many of them disappear when you play on television. You are not trying to get across to a (hopefully) large and (hopefully) understanding audience. Instead, you're not really playing to anybody – or you're playing to an anonymous group of people who could be anywhere, in the North, in London, in Japan or the States. You don't know whether they are listening or not, because they're not there. And with the television Shakespeares, were they all recorded?'

'Yes', said Moshinsky.

'Nothing went out live? Well, in that case each scene will be taken away and cut, and you might be asked to produce minuscule bits of the text at any given moment. You may have to re-take. Scenes may be taken out of order. We were discussing this morning Ophelia's soliloquy after Hamlet has berated her. Well, you might have to do that soliloquy before Hamlet actually berates you. He might be berating you in three days' time, or have berated you two days before. You have got to be able to recall the context exactly. That's a lot of pressure. And all the lights are there, and the weird machinery, all around you, all the time, and you have to create in your mind the kind of acting space that you feel automatically if you are appearing behind a proscenium arch or anywhere in the live theatre.'

'Comedy', said the first speaker, 'must be very difficult.'

'Comedy', said Moshinsky, 'is sort of impossible.'

ELIJAH MOSHINSKY: The discipline that television imposes on the actor can have a good and positive effect. You can't *generalize* on television. You would be surprised at the extent to which actors generalize in Shakespeare. They get passages which build up in the writing and they get carried away with the sound of their voices. It was interesting to do *Coriolanus* with Alan Howard, who had previously played it in an expressionistic RSC production, directed by Terry Hands. Alan Howard's strong point is letting go, seizing the passion of the moment, and for television, we had to make sure that he was being absolutely accurate. It is not a matter of scaling performances down for television, but of making sure that the actor is being absolutely specific, because the camera finds out any kind of vagueness and that curious stentorian voice that you sometimes don't notice in the theatre but always makes you turn off the television.

The directors on the Shakespeare series were always discussing this question of space. How could we get the best space on the screen which would fit into the space where we imagined that people would be looking at it? After all, we were asking people to sit down in front of a television for, say, three hours, continuously. I very rarely do that myself. The phone rings, the baby cries. It's not easy to watch a television set for three hours. And so you had to develop a technique which was as strong as an actor's technique in the theatre, to intrigue an audience. And, of course, what intrigues me might not intrigue millions of viewers. Incidentally, the viewing figures on the Shakespeares averaged at about three million per programme. That's really quite amazing.

'In the House of Commons the other day', I mentioned, 'the Labour MP, Tony Banks, said that Shakespeare would naturally have written for television, if he'd been alive today, because he would have looked for the largest possible audience. But could he have written in the same way for that audience, if he didn't know who they were or what were their likes and dislikes? If you have to record a play in bits and pieces, as we've heard, and not within the story sequence, this prevents not just comic timing but that flow of performance which can bear actors along to rhetorical heights. It also prevents actors from carrying the audience with them right into the heart of the play, that *rapprochement* that sometimes exists in the live theatre.'

ELIJAH MOSHINSKY: That problem doesn't exist for most television programmes because the content and the technique is scaled to the medium. But it does exist for Shakespeare on television because that is where the through-line is vital. I take interpretation of Shakespeare to mean your understanding of the text as a whole and the way in which you see how your own role is developing, if you are an actor, or how the scene is developing, if you are a director, all the way through; and it's very hard to calculate the pitch of the performance if you're taking the scenes apart, take by take, and not playing them sequentially.

But I do think it is possible to rehearse a Shakespeare play for television in such a way that the actors know whether they're coming in or going out and roughly the pitch of their performances. But this takes time. At least it takes more than four weeks. I found it so difficult within the time available to cope with so many plots, and the dense language, and the things that would not knit together. . . .

'How did you cope with the problem', I asked, 'of plays written in language designed for a staging which lacked the pictorial opportunities of television?'

ELIJAH MOSHINSKY: Yes, there were too many pictorial opportunities. This problem was made more difficult by the theory current at the time to have very bare stages. The philosophy was that you should empty the stage and let the audience fix the imagery with you. You had to develop the pictorial imagination by working with the audience and the bare space.

One of the great successes, when the BBC series started, was Trevor Nunn's studio *Macbeth*, with Ian McKellen and Judi Dench. And that, of course, was televised, by independent television. They took fourteen days as opposed to our six, and they had the benefit of all the previous rehearsals. But it was interesting to see how the mannerisms which worked in the theatre came over on the small screen, the odd speech patterns and so on. Perhaps television encourages a different sense of reality.

There was another problem. When you do a Shakespeare at the BBC, you get issued with a designer. The BBC is an enormous factory and it has these in-house set and costume designers. If you're going to do something which is scheduled for the studio in week 37, they look up the list and see who's free for week 37; and you may get a designer who normally works for the Paul Daniels Show. Or they may take someone off *EastEnders* who can be put to work designing the costumes for *Love's Labour's Lost*. And the director has to communicate his interpretation to people who do not normally bother with Illyria. The result was that you got these naff and very silly visualizations of important and poetic situations. Close-ups were a great help.

If, in the future, television gets round to Shakespeare again, the plays should be done on film, not on video tape, and independently from a large bureaucracy and more time should be given to the work of each production so that such problems don't pre-empt the artistic judgements.

But now it's not economically viable.

'Is there also a quality difference', asked a member of the audience, 'between film and video? Or do you want to use film simply to avoid the bureaucracy?'

ELIJAH MOSHINSKY: It's really to prevent one from being stuck in the studio. There is still a qualitative difference between video on location and video in the studio. If you work on film, you can move, as Zeffirelli did with his *Otello*, from location in Cyprus back to the studio and on to some other location. With film, you have much more flexibility.

But if you are doing films for television, the primary element is still the actor's face. On television there is a gain in psychological allusiveness and in anything which has to do with feelings of self-destruction or indeed with those existential emotions, man alone and pondering his future.

But there is a tremendous loss with anything which has to do with irony. In directing Shakespeare, I found that the insoluble problems always came in scenes that depended on somebody overhearing someone else saying something, because in that kind of situation the audience has to know where the people are.

In television, you have no sense of geography, of spatial gaps. If you shoot from one angle a person's face, and then shift the angle of vision by 30 per cent, you do not know from what part of the room you are watching that face. You simply know that you are seeing it from a different angle. And so if you give an overall shot, and have the chap behind a haystack listening, the result looks unbelievably stagey, like a kind of primitive Feydeau farce.

The other point about television, as opposed to film, is that the television image is made up of electronic dots hitting a piece of glass; and so if you make that image smaller on the screen, you have an enormous loss of quality. When somebody is very small on a screen, that image has been registered by some fifty or sixty dots. This is why close-ups are so much more powerful than distance shots, which can be so beautifully achieved on film. In *Dr Zhivago*, you have these wonderful scenes of a tiny figure against a vast landscape. You can do that on film, but not on video. In television, you are primarily dealing with the cross-cutting of close-ups. But television does gain with soliloquies and monologues, where the character is looking inward and considering what to do next. That was why it was so much easier to do *Coriolanus* than *A Midsummer Night's Dream*.

'What about the cutting of the text?' I asked.

ELIJAH MOSHINSKY: I was the first person on the series to start cutting the text, because one of the holy writs until then was that nothing should be cut. I started cutting discreetly, altering the rhythms of scenes which seemed fractionally too long for television, to make the presentation more forceful; but when I came to *Coriolanus*, I decided to be bolder. You have to take a decision on that play. You either direct it as an epic play about a political debate or as a study of an alienated state of mind, which is how I chose to do it. The study in alienation is rarely brought out in an epic production, although it is one of the strong ingredients in the play and one particularly suitable for television. I cut the play to highlight my point of view and what I regarded as the strengths of the medium; but there was no technical necessity to do so.

It aroused a critical storm, but I had to make that experiment because the presentation of Shakespeare on television had become weak and middle-brow and lacking in force and seriousness. The rhythms of presentation had become limp; and the only thing to do was to handle the text so that parts would be highlighted, parts muted or placed in the background. It was necessary to give the television version a definite shape, instead of handling each scene in the same undifferentiated way. But that meant losing the epic dimension of *Coriolanus*, which infuriated some people. I got hate mail, interestingly enough more from the United States rather than in England where they seemed to accept this more highly developed approach. In America, they thought it sacrilegious.

The director Maurice Stewart, who was in the audience, suggested that Shakespeare would have cut and changed his own plays, if he'd been writing for television; and if we just present the full Shakespearian text, we lose the theatricality on television which comes with the stage performance. 'What Moshinsky is suggesting is that you should manipulate the material to recreate a similar energy to that which has been lost. We are, after all, just telling a story.'

'But narrative on television', answered Moshinsky, 'works quite differently from narrative on the stage. Do you remember that survey where schoolchildren were asked, after they'd watched the News, what they could remember of it? They could remember hardly anything, fifteen minutes later, virtually nothing. One of the strengths of television is the constant present, which is also its weakness if you are trying to build up a narrative structure. In a theatre, the space stays the same when different actors enter and leave the stage, and so a sense of continuity develops through the fixed relationship between the audience and the stage. But on television, it's just a constant present: "This is Rome", "This is a battlefield", "This is in someone's mind!", and the feeling conveyed is one of flashing action. The narrative becomes like a mosaic.'

'In Algeria', I pointed out, 'and throughout North Africa and the Arab

124

countries, they have storytellers who come in from the desert, at about nine o'clock in the morning, and tell these long stories in verse or rhythmic prose, for perhaps two or three hours at a time, epic and religious stories, sometimes broken up by songs. And people listen to them and take back these stories to their families, and re-tell them, word-perfectly. They are trained to remember these stories and the actual words through which they have been expressed. Shakespeare's audiences too were brought up in an oral culture, where the actual nature of the language trained the mind to receive and to remember the whole story. But on television, you can never do that. People will never watch television without being interrupted by something, whether it's a phone call or a commercial; and we aren't trained in the oral tradition or to remember. Doesn't this mean that the quality of the experience is diminished?'

'The single play is a dying art form on TV', pointed out a member of the audience, while another suggested that Shakespeare might have preferred the mini-series anyway.

'I don't think it's necessarily true to say', intervened a third, 'that television is primarily a visual medium. If you watch people looking at *Coronation Street*, they don't watch it all the time. They just notice where the scene is set – in *The Rovers*, for example – and then they listen to what is said. They might even turn the volume up and leave the room to make a cup of tea. Once the setting has been established, it's not necessary to look any more.'

'The real difference between television and the theatre', argued another, 'is that you tend to watch television by yourself or with a few members of your family, whereas watching the theatre is always a social activity. I can't watch Shakespeare on TV because the plays are so public. The only one I managed to watch was Terry Hands' *Macbeth*, because it was so intimate, just faces, no scenery distractions. I concentrate much better in the theatre.'

I invited the Polish theatre critic and author, Dr Andrzej Zurowski, to comment. Dr Zurowski works for television in Gdansk; and Polish theatre is noted for its visual excitement. But do these images translate well into television?

ANDRZEJ ZUROWSKI: On Polish television we have about eighty new drama productions every year. On every Monday evening, there is a new production of a play. We have many types of plays, both contemporary and classics. But we do not usually attempt Shakespeare, who is very popular on the Polish stage, but not on television; and when we do try to televise Shakespeare, it's not very successful. But we do receive the BBC Shakespeares and they are very popular. But don't you think that television is really a very dangerous place for Shakespeare? I get quite afraid for him. Television is a very naturalistic, or realistic, medium. If I understand Shakespeare, he doesn't really like naturalism very much. It's not just because he worked on a empty stage at the Globe, it's because all the pedantry of naturalism wasn't necessary for him.

But the BBC Shakespeares did try to be naturalistic. I mean, there were real castles and so on. You don't need a real castle in the background for Shakespeare. This type of visualization of the text reminded me of the nineteenth-century operatic conventions, and frankly, Shakespeare is not a good opera singer.

The Shakespearian translator, Jean-Michel Déprats, intervened to disagree with Dr Zurowski.

JEAN-MICHEL DÉPRATS: Forgive me if I speak about cinema and television in the same breath, because I know they don't work in the same way, but I can think of at least two cases where Shakespeare on the screen left more scope for the imagination than usually happens in the theatre. These were Orson Welles' *Othello* and Moshinsky's *All's Well That Ends Well*. They may have been exceptions but they're strong enough to disprove your general rule that television is a more realistic medium than the stage, because you can work with real sets. It is true that I wasn't convinced by the use of natural landscapes in the BBC's *As You Like It*, but this was because the medium was used so badly.

I don't think that you can ever say that television is necessarily more realistic than the theatre. There are as many conventions and codes in the cinema and television as in the theatre, but they're different ones. The space left for the imagination in Moshinsky's *All's Well* is very important and it proved that you can use television creatively.

Orson Welles' *Othello* was filmed on location and in a real castle. But the fact that it is filmed in a castle doesn't make it more realistic or leave less scope for the imagination. Nor is there necessarily any discrepancy between Shakespeare's text and the image of a real object, the castle. It all depends on the relationship between the text and the image. If that relationship is not merely illustrative, that is, representational in a very narrow sense, then the medium is not purely naturalistic.

The Greek director Stavros Doufexis wanted to agree and disagree with Déprats and Moshinsky. 'Yes', he said, 'we have had some good Shakespeare films, very few, but they can't be ignored. But I have also seen some of these BBC Shakespeares! I do not think that television as a medium can cope with Shakespeare. If Shakespeare were living now, I think he would write for television, but in a very different way . . .'

'Why would Shakespeare have written for television?' asked Moshinsky. 'There are playwrights who don't. The theatre isn't dead because television exists.'

'Well, I don't know Shakespeare personally', continued Doufexis, 'but I think he would, because he liked to try out every possibility, and television is a very big possibility. But putting Shakespeare's plays as they have been written on television reduces them. They lose a little, as classical Greek plays lose. I have that problem now. I was asked to do a series of videos of Greek traditional comedies, and for the first time, I said, "All right!" Now when I am asked, I take a little bit longer before saying "Yes" because I think to myself, "How can I produce in those cassettes the special magic that we need for tragedy, the special theatrical magic?" That is also the problem with Shakespeare. Perhaps it can be done, because there have been those exceptional films. But I still think that Shakespeare loses . . .'

ELIJAH MOSHINSKY: One of the reasons why I described how the BBC series was actually brought together was to suggest that the faults lay not in the medium itself but in the great broadcasting bureaucracy that distorts the medium. If you're working with a system where you can't pick your own design team and have to squeeze into impossible schedules, naturally things go wrong. The medium itself hasn't really been tested.

But I do think that there are better Shakespeare plays for television and worse ones. *All's Well* works well because it is introspective: *A Midsummer Night's Dream* is much more difficult because in the last section, you are supposed to be watching a play within a play and that's a very difficult idea to capture on television. Comedy is difficult, irony is difficult, word-play is difficult. And unfortunately, on television there is none of the mystery and suspense that you get in the theatre as the house lights dim . . .

127

An actor in the audience intervened: 'But when Shakespeare wrote those plays, people would be selling oranges in the theatre and cutting purses, and the audiences would be treating the stage with as much irreverence as we now treat television. As an actor, I was quite impressed by the BBC Shakespeares, because I thought the enterprise would have been doomed to failure from Day One. So much in the theatre depends on the actors manipulating the audience, which you can't do on television. And the plays are constructed in an almost cinematic way, with short scenes, moving from place to place. Shakespeare writes in a way which does not mean that the audience has to pay reverent attention all the time to what is going on, although, admittedly, if the Russians invaded Poland in the interval, it might be a bit of a distraction.'

'It's difficult enough', said Moshinsky, 'to do any Shakespeare play well. This was where Trevor Nunn's studio *Macbeth* was such an interesting test case, because the performers had discovered the play so well and the camera simply picked up what they had discovered. That cuts across all the problems of the medium, simply to have a cast who know and interpret the play exactly, and then you just have to photograph what they are doing.'

'There is almost as great a gap', I said, 'between the staging of Shakespeare's plays in the original Globe Theatre and in the Barbican, as there is between the Barbican and television. Shakespeare worked under conditions which were more like Peter Brook's rough theatre than his empty space.'

ELIJAH MOSHINSKY: When you ask the question, 'Is Shakespeare our contemporary?' you are really striking at the heart of the problem. You obviously can't ignore the past and forget the differences between then and now. And you can't forget what has happened between then and now, just as when listening to Wagner, it's hard to forget how a particular tune was used by the Nazis. But at the same time, what Shakespeare's audiences saw were modern plays; and what directors have to find is some kind of way in which the plays today can seem equally immediate and modern. Sometimes this happens when a Shakespeare play touches on a subject which has its contemporary equivalent; and sometimes it happens if you can handle the subject in a modern style.

When we were planning *All's Well*, we looked at the films of Cocteau, because I felt that the play lived in a world of its own. It was semi-fantasy. We wanted a dream-like entrance into another world, an imagined, domestic, seventeenth-century world; and we discovered one technical point from Cocteau's films, his use of the long, tracking shot. The camera would move for ten minutes in one long single shot, which is what you sometimes have to do if you don't want to use a lot of film. In *La Belle et la Bête*, which was made just after the war when film stock was low, Cocteau used these wonderful, long, tracking movements, and we used the same device in *All's Well*, starting from behind the scene and moving into it, very slowly, bringing the audience with us.

It was a very deliberate technique, to keep the camera always moving, but very, very slowly, so that the scene is always getting slightly larger or being captured from a different angle. This was one way to bridge the gap between the world of the plays and the modern audience, between the fable and today's fact. It had to be a historical setting. Even if they all wore modern dress, it wouldn't have helped. The trick lay in finding a style and a technique to draw the audience into the fantasy.

ANDRZEJ ZUROWSKI: I would like to return for a moment to this subject of realism, because, of course, I don't want to say that realism is the only way in which you can approach television Shakespeares. It is just very tempting to show real chariots if you have that opportunity; and in the BBC series, the temptation wasn't as a whole resisted. You found a way of bringing together the poetical, metaphorical style of Shakespeare with a television style, but others didn't; and even with your style, the effect was to reduce Shakespeare.

For example, in *Julius Caesar*, you don't have to see Rome, because the questions in *Julius Caesar* are not simply Roman ones. If Shakespeare wants to be my contemporary, he must speak with me here, not in ancient Rome; and if he doesn't, then he is an interesting museum piece – and the best place for a museum piece is a museum, not television.

ELIJAH MOSHINSKY: Yes, you're right, but helping Shakespeare to be our contemporary is not just a matter of putting the actors in modern dress. It is a much larger

129

problem and it changes all the time. Shakespeare should be done on television, because he is the greatest playwright and what he has to say must be made to communicate. It is just a matter of unlocking the means of communication. Shakespeare is difficult on television, not just for reasons of realism, but just because the language is slower and the pace of unravelling plots. It just has a different tempo from normal television viewing.

'When you say, *just*', I intervened, 'that's an enormous word! For an enormous problem!'

ELIJAH MOSHINSKY: Yes, it's a problem. Look at the basic structure of a Shakespeare play. Three or four plots usually have to be established in the first twenty minutes. For television, that's too long. You start with plot A, and quickly go on to plots B, C and D, before returning to plot A twenty minutes later, when people will have forgotten. Curiously enough, your only response is that the basic structure somehow creaks when you see it on television.

And so it is not just a question of awful design, of *papier mâché* castles, and that sort of thing. It's also a matter of internal structure. What you have to do is to find a structure so that the dilemmas of the play can come across on television.

'I'm going to express this point rather badly', I said, and proceeded to do so. 'Poor Shakespeare productions stick to the narrative line rather doggedly, but when Shakespeare is done well, you can feel how he is exploring the moral inscape of a scene, often in a leisurely way. Take, for example, that enormous debate scene in *Troilus and Cressida* about the nature of order in society. For that scene to work, you need a close involvement between the speakers and the audience, so that we all can follow the twists and turns in the reasoning. And you also need some commonly accepted moral framework within which the discussions can take place, although it could be constantly challenged, as it is in *Troilus and Cressida*. That framework is partly conditioned by our understanding as to how the world and the universe are physically constructed. In this instance, the Ptolemaic structure is roughly accepted by Shakespeare and his audience, with the sun and the moon enthroned in the heavens as the King and his Consort are enthroned on earth. If you accept this hierarchical pattern, then you can argue within it. You can use the framework to explore dimensions of the plot which are not necessarily narrative dimensions, but spiritual and moral ones – if we mean by "moral", what someone *ought* to do under these circumstances. But on television, we are conditioned to thinking in terms of short scenes, developing a plot in a fairly clear line. If a television writer presented something like Ulysses' speech in that order debate in *Troilus and Cressida*, he would get very black looks from his director. It's too long. The second act is too long – and much too static. No chance of getting a slot, no chance of getting resources, it just wouldn't fit. And I suspect that it isn't just a case of not being suitable for television, but of not fitting into our ways of thought today at all.'

There was a polite pause.

'Did they', asked a member of the audience, 'do any surveys? How many ordinary people watched the Shakespeares on television of their own accord?'

'They did audience surveys', said Moshinsky, 'all the time. The average viewing figure, as I have said, was about three million people, which was considered very low. But if you think of this in relationship to the numbers who would go to a RSC production, it was an incredible hit. There was also a social breakdown of these figures which indicated, although I can't remember the details, that it was largely watched by those who go to the theatre. There wasn't the cross-over of interest between the theatre-goers and the non-theatre-goers, as we had hoped.'

'The main purpose', the questioner replied, 'of putting Shakespeare on television is not just to get bigger audiences, but to bring him back into contact with the ordinary people who would have seen his plays in his own time. And if that didn't happen – well . . .'

ELIJAH MOSHINSKY: One of the nice things that you can do with Shakespeare on television is to debunk that aura of pretentiousness which often surrounds Shakespearian productions. I actually can't watch Shakespeare on television, but I have a great deal of difficulty in watching him on the stage as well. The fact is that it is very rare to see a good Shakespeare production in any medium. You go along and hope that the production will unlock some particular truth or intensity, but the result very rarely comes up to the potential. Only the performer can put across the meanings within the play to the audience. The director can help, but the task is really that of the performers. The main directorial problem is to get the right actors together at the right time. All other aesthetic questions are subordinate to that task.

'What doesn't work well on television', said an actor in the audience, 'is spectacle, the glorious heritage approach. What does work well is soap: *Dynasty*, *Dallas*, *The Colbys*. They're all the same, because they're about the pain of relationships, and intrigue, and of powerful people who do terrible things to one another. And Shakespeare writes wonderful soap, but we haven't noticed that he does, because he's always surrounded by Our Glorious Heritage.'

Maurice Stewart agreed. 'I've had headmasters coming in while I'm rehearsing a Shakespeare play and saying, "I do hope it's going to be a proper Shakespeare!" meaning the kind of production he saw when he was growing up thirty years ago. I think that the BBC have done Shakespeare a disservice with these glossy videos with the *Time-Life* imprimatur. They're formula-ridden, they're packaged so that you can pick them from the shelf in Tesco's, and we're going to be lumbered with them for the next twenty years. My students in America go down to the media-centre in their well-heeled university and they pull out Reinhardt's *A Midsummer Night's Dream* and Olivier's *Othello*, and they sit down on cushions, loll back, stupefied, and let the stuff wash over them.'

'The real difference', said Moshinsky, 'between television and the theatre *is* the way in which it is received. There is no direct link between the communicators and the viewers. The process of delivery has become fragmented, made according to certain bureaucratic formulas, packaged into cassettes, received as an item on a university syllabus. Of course, the play can still be read, but I don't agree with those academics who say that *King Lear* can never be performed. You can never really reproduce popular drama of the past on television, because you can never reproduce the circumstances in which the plays were originally conceived. You have to find some other way of making Shakespeare our contemporary. Having said that, I do think that the BBC performed a service in attempting to produce Shakespeare for television. They did him a disservice by not rising sufficiently to the challenge.'

'When Shakespeare was alive,' said an actor in the audience, 'the acting company had the power over the production. They owned the building, they commissioned the playwright and got progress reports from him, and they were responsible for the final result. That situation continued until the turn of this century, when they started to lose power to the directors, and since then, and particularly over the past thirty or forty years, an actor has had to work through some director's academic concept of the play to reach his audience. Television and other mechanical media have distanced the actor from the audience still further; and I think that the answer is to minimize the distance as best you can. People watch *Dynasty* and *Dallas* because of the actors. They love Joan Collins, they love Howard Keel. They don't watch the writing, they don't notice the design, they don't

132

bother about the directors or the producers. Because actors have lost power within the theatre, we have lost the dynamic in Shakespeare's plays.'

'I have always thought', said Moshinsky, 'that a director ought to enhance the communication between the actor and the audience. John Elsom's point is important. When you're tackling Shakespeare, you are not just dealing with plays from an ordinary playwright. You're dealing with a total world view, a world view that has been partly lost to us, but if we can start to recover it, great riches of insight open out to us in the most extraordinary way. It's not possible for Shakespeare's plays to be watched, as if you were reading a magazine article. You require a lot of self-preparation and self-education to bring yourself to the point where you can take it all in. It took me years of theatre-going and thinking about Shakespeare before I could feel at home with certain Shakespeare plays; and for my generation, the person who opened up Shakespeare was Peter Brook. And I haven't seen anything quite so good since.'

'Are you saying', asked a member of the audience, 'that it's not television material?'

'No', said Moshinsky, 'I'm saying that it's not easily transferable to television. You can't just film a Shakespeare play as if it were a television script; and the medium itself is not as accessible to directorial techniques as is the theatre. You can put on a Shakespeare play anywhere. You only need four people and a room, and some people to come to see it, and that's a kind of production. But to produce Shakespeare on television, you have to have a certain production capacity, which means the patronage of some enormous organization, like the BBC. I have personally always found that patronage to be double-edged. It helps you and it destroys you.'

'Isn't the assumption that Shakespeare should work on television', I asked, 'tied up with the idea that if he's any good, then he *must* be our contemporary? Perhaps the reverse is the case. Perhaps Shakespeare is too good to be our contemporary and that we're not up to him. Critical fashions do change. In the 1690s, under the influence of the French, we thought that Shakespeare was a talented barbarian who needed to be tidied up. In the 1790s, under the influence of the Germans, we thought that he was immortal and had some kind of divine access to those primary human emotions that Racine had overlooked, and then in the 1960s, Jan Kott came along and said he was topical, and we started to look for the topicality in Shakespeare. And because he's topical, he has to work on television. And he doesn't. If we pursue this line, we are in danger of misunderstanding what Shakespeare actually has to say and this could be actually a great challenge to us, because it upsets all of our ideas. Everybody seems to think that a play must be more democratic if it's seen by three million people, but you do need a big centralized bureaucracy

133

to put it on, and that may not be a very democratic way of doing things. Everybody says, "You've got to have Shakespeare on television because he reaches this wide audience", but reach it at what level? With what quality of understanding? That is what matters. I think that we are trying to package Shakespeare to suit our particular tastes and our life-styles. This is where I agree with Maurice Stewart. We are not doing Shakespeare a great service.'

'But Shakespeare has to be accessible', commented a member of the audience.

'Of course', I said, 'but not *made* accessible at any cost.'

Here Marianne Ackerman from Canada intervened. 'What would be the response if somebody sat down for a year with *Macbeth*, and took the play apart, and re-assembled it again with the particular qualities of television in mind? Perhaps he wouldn't want to call it *Macbeth*, because the outcry would be so enormous. The value of Shakespeare doesn't lie in the form or the styles of acting; and it doesn't solely lie in the systems of belief in Shakespeare's times. He has something to say, just as the Bible has something to say, even though we may live in a secular society. Can't you unpack Shakespeare and parcel him up again for television?'

'Yes, I think you can,' said Moshinsky. 'That's what Verdi did with *Othello*. He transformed it totally into a nineteenth-century opera. But that wasn't our brief. We had to perform Shakespeare. We couldn't tear the plays apart, extract the innards and create new bodies for them. That's why perhaps the medium hasn't yet seriously got to grips with Shakespeare. What you need is a producer, as distinct from a director, who will ask you to explore the ways and means of televising *Macbeth*; but the technical means have been so inaccessible until now, only available to state organizations. This situation though is changing. Five years ago, it was impossible just to pick up a camera and make a video cassette of something. Now anybody can do it. Now, you can edit video more precisely than you can film. This means that you can do smaller and less official productions; and, of course, that means that you can experiment.'

Two theatre critics in the audience, Michael Handelsaltz from Israel and Caroline Alexander from France, intervened.

MICHAEL HANDELSALTZ: There is a proverb in my language which may not translate into English, which is, that you can lead a horse to water, but you cannot force him to drink. If you are producing Shakespeare on television, you are bringing water to the horse, which is even more generous, but you still can't force him to drink or to enjoy the water when drinking. You can go to a lot of effort to make Shakespeare accessible to people, but some of them will still turn the set

134

off after five minutes. You've got to catch them and hold them until the end of the show, and they can switch off a television set more easily than they can leave a theatre.

CAROLINE ALEXANDER: You can also say that opera doesn't suit television. In France, we have a great admiration for the BBC Shakespeares, because until now, none of our channels have presented the complete cycle of Molière's plays. Roger Planchon is now apparently going to do them for Channel Three. But the BBC Shakespeares were all seen on Channel Three. Of course, something may be lost, but I can remember when Patrice Chéreau's production of *The Ring* at Bayreuth was televised in August, which is the worst month, and it had an audience of something like three or four million people. Well, it may be a small percentage of the population, but that's an enormous figure. And were they all opera lovers? And a televised Shakespeare has one big advantage. It leaves a trace. You can repeat it. It is a witness for the future. No theatre production leaves a trace.

'The response from France', said Moshinsky, 'was very enthusiastic. I actually gave a seminar in France on *All's Well* and to my surprise, everybody had seen it. I get letters from France and the States, mainly very grateful ones, from people who would not have had a chance of seeing Shakespeare otherwise ...'

'In the Middle East', said Michael Handelsaltz, 'it was broadcast by Jordanian TV and we picked up the signal ...'

'The dissemination', said Moshinsky, 'was fantastic. But in Britain, it was felt that the productions weren't deep enough and the performances could have been improved ...'

'I'm getting a bit impatient', said an educationalist, Leon Rogers, in the audience, 'with all these negative remarks about the BBC series. It all depends on how you use them. In an educational institute like mine, we don't just plonk the thing on a video and say, "Right, we're going to watch *King Lear* today." We talk about *King Lear* first and we may see another version, such as Olivier's *Lear*. There is an enormous value in being able to take them down from a shelf and look at them; and I don't think that you should dismiss an audience of three million in Britain!'

'It's probably better to watch it on cassette', said Moshinsky, 'than on transmission. You can study it on a cassette. But the artistic problems remain the same. You can't direct a Shakespeare play in a medium for which it was not intended in six days.'

'Marianne Ackerman suggested that we should "unpack" Shakespeare and reassemble him for television', I said. 'But perhaps we should go further, and use Shakespeare as a springboard for our own imaginations to leap on to other subjects. It is always much easier to find the money to bring acknowledged classics to mass markets, particularly through an organization like the BBC, than it is for directors and writers to raise the cash for projects of their own. If we'd have had the same system in Shakespeare's time, then the money would have gone to videos of Seneca, Plautus and Terence, and Shakespeare would have had to wait for years for the right kind of support. Shakespeare relied on classical authors a great deal, but he used them as a starting point for his own creativity.'

'When you put Shakespeare on stage', said Michael Handelsaltz, 'you don't change or alter the text, which remains to be read. A terrible production can be forgotten. But if you put him on tape, there is a definite product, which stays there as a kind of continual record. Students will look at it and their ideas about the text will be altered because they're looking at a permanent model. In that sense, you can be more free with a stage version because it's more transitory. You can cut it, or change it, or use it as a springboard for your own ideas. Nobody is going to take it down from the shelf in an educational institution.'

'But the text is still there', said Moshinsky.

'You're right about using Shakespeare as a springboard', agreed a member of the audience. 'The writers of *Dynasty* said that they had based the first three series on stories about the Borgias. If Shakespeare wasn't so famous, and this wonderful fund of material suddenly emerged, then somebody might have got hold of the rights, as they did with Robert Graves' *I, Claudius* and *Claudius the God,* and got together the best writers and directors to adapt it for television without so much reverence. And more people might have watched it. The name of Shakespeare on the package might well have reduced the numbers who wanted to see the series.'

Marianne Ackerman and Jean-Michel Déprats both disagreed. 'A lot of people want to see Shakespeare, certainly in Canada', said Marianne Ackerman, 'and seeing a competent production of Shakespeare on television can't be worse than seeing a good stage production from a bad seat in the theatre, which is how most people watch Shakespeare.' 'Lots of people in France discovered Shakespeare through that series', said Déprats, 'even people who don't know English. They watched the series because they wanted to listen to the music of the language. They had subtitles, of course; and they loved the plots.'

'Could that be intellectual snobbery?' I asked.

'Not in France', Déprats answered. 'But I think that it's wrong to talk about the series as a whole and to generalize about Shakespeare for television. There were some great artistic successes in the series and several disasters. I simply couldn't watch *The Tempest*, with that terrible cardboard set. It wasn't alive, it wasn't good television and the director did not know what to do with the play.'

'One production of *Much Ado*', said Moshinsky, 'was so bad that it had to be scrapped. I found a cassette of it once and it was very funny. They had to do the play again, which is why it was the last of the series.'

'I thought what was wrong with the BBC Shakespeares', said a member of the audience, 'was that they often looked as if they were televised version of stage plays, as if someone had placed a camera in front of a proscenium arch set, with a palm tree sticking out of the wings because it was supposed to be Cyprus.'

ELIJAH MOSHINSKY: Working in the television studio is like being half-way between a small theatre and a film set. We talked a lot about the way in which the studio should be handled, but time was always the problem. The staginess that you mentioned is partly because we didn't have time to do the number of shots that you normally would use in a film.

Let's suppose that we were filming a very simple action, such as my picking up that glass of water and drinking it. In a film, you would have a shot of the glass, a shot of my hand going out to pick it up, a shot of my drinking it. But in a television studio, there would be a camera that would simply follow the action. You wouldn't have the number or variety of shots that would be normal in a film. That's one reason why it looks as if you are filming a stage action. You are not using the conventions of film.

Eventually I found out that the camera could be my friend in televising Shakespeare, because it could be selective. If you had a duologue scene, you could sometimes see both people, but you could sometimes just look at the speaker, or the listener, or something else altogether. On the stage, you can't do that so easily. You can't select what the audience should be seeing. But again it depends on the number of shots. If you're limited in the number of shots you can use, you photograph the studio picture with only a little cross-cutting.

There is also a problem with speech rhythms. The longer the speeches, the harder they are to handle in television terms.

I wanted to lift the plays a little out of reality, in the most gentle way, by being very naturalistic or very historical, to make Shakespeare, as it were, a little less of a contemporary. At Stratford these days, there is a tendency to do the opposite, to change Shakespeare's speech rhythms to bring them closer to those of today. I found that it was better to make the play, not abstract exactly, but to lift it out of anything which seemed banal and everyday. Much of this had to do with the manipulation of close-ups, so that you were not too concerned with the surrounding world; but there was always a danger of becoming static, of losing the sense of action. Once you start to go down that path of no action, you're in danger of arriving at reverie. And it is very hard to judge, how to create action on glass in a box.

You don't have that problem in modern plays for many reasons, but if you look at *Dallas* or *Dynasty*, there's very little action. You mainly see portrait shots. The problem of action on television is not shared by film, because you can cut and manipulate the medium to arrive at a dynamic movement. And in televising Shakespeare, there are some plays where the sense of reverie is appropriate and others where it is not.

'You said that television doesn't suit comedy', stated a member of the audience, 'but I saw John Cleese in *The Taming of the Shrew* and that utterly succeeded.'

'I was thinking about the more artificial comedies', said Moshinsky, 'such as *Twelfth Night*, *A Midsummer Night's Dream* or *Love's Labour's Lost*. You don't know on television how audiences are taking complex, linguistic jokes or ironical situations where people overhear one another. Magic poses another question. On television, it's so easy to make visual tricks, but if you fall for those, you lose the sense of magic in the script. You can have Puck appearing and disappearing as often you like, but if you indulge in that sort of trickery, you lose the relationship between the fairy world and the mortal kingdom. Conjuring tricks are much more effective on the stage, because you can't see how they're done. On television, you have so many easy ways of deceiving that the magic loses the sense of utter astonishment. And Shakespeare himself, of course, speaks in a somewhat derogatory way of the Italian masques of the time, and the new mechanization that was then being introduced.'

'In that case', came the inevitable question, 'if Shakespeare had have been our contemporary, would he have written for television?'

'If Shakespeare were our contemporary', replied Moshinsky, 'which I have always found an impossible thought, I can't imagine that he would resist any great opportunity. He would have thought about the medium, absorbed it and learnt how to focus it, which was what he did with the theatre of his time.'

IS SHAKESPEARE A FEUDAL
PROPAGANDIST?

with
**Alexander Anikst, Ruby Cohn, Erich Fried,
David Hare, Hugh Quarshie,
Ernst Schumacher, Richard Wilson and,
in the chair, Ian Herbert**

The horror of social disorder runs throughout Shakespeare's canon – from the early tragedies, *Titus Andronicus* and *Romeo and Juliet*, to the history plays and the tragedies of his maturity, until the final tragi-comedies, including the last play of all, *The Tempest*. It even surfaces in light-hearted, romantic comedies, such as *Much Ado About Nothing* or *As You Like It*.

No Shakespearian subject could be more contemporary. There are societies in different stages of collapse all around the world. And violence is not only as 'American as apple pie', it is also more British than cricket and more German than *Lederhosen*. We have various theories as to why societies fall apart, through envy, social injustice, class conflicts, and plain wickedness, many of which Shakespeare would share.

But Shakespeare also puts forward the vision of an orderly society with a 'natural' hierarchy, mirroring that of the Ptolemaic heavens, with the king enthroned like a sun, with courtiers who obey his will and with authority transmitted from the crown to all who live in the realm. One clear expression of this hierarchical order occurs in one of Shakespeare's most disillusioned plays, *Troilus and Cressida*, where, in the first act, Ulysses calls for social discipline among the Greek troops:

> O! when degree is shak'd,
> Which is the ladder of all high designs,
> The enterprise is sick! How could communities,
> Degrees in schools, and brotherhoods in cities,
> Peaceful commerce from dividable shores,
> The primogenive and due of birth,
> Prerogative of age, crowns, sceptres, laurels,
> But by degree, stand in authentic place?

140

Take but degree away, untune that string,
And hark! what discord follows!

(I.iii.101)

In passages like these, Shakespeare is not just paying tactful compliments
to the Crown. He is defending feudalism as a natural law of the universe.

This law also imposed moral duties to the effect that men and women
should not rebel against the stations in life in which they have been
placed; and it applies as much to King Lear, who gave up his regal duties
while trying to retain the dignity of being a king, as it does to Henry
Bolingbroke who overthrew his king, Richard II. Nowadays, the thought
that you should keep within your assigned class and should not aspire
beyond it, seems both primitive and repressive; and Brecht is not the only
writer to insist that in such matters Shakespeare revealed himself not just
as a man of his age but also a propagandist for an unfair system.

Brecht's friend and biographer, Dr Ernst Schumacher, a professor at
Humboldt University, East Berlin, was on the panel of speakers for this
session which was held in the Young Vic's main theatre. In the chair was
the editor and publisher of *London Theatre Record*, Ian Herbert, who
invited the black actor, Hugh Quarshie, to open the discussion.

*

HUGH QUARSHIE: Whether we regard Shakespeare as a feudal
propagandist or as the source of many of the libertarian,
humanist values which make up the liberal tradition is a
matter of interpretation.

We should start by sorting out the confusion between
history, or versions of history, and nature. I hold 'myth' to
be a version of history that's been elevated into the status
of a law of nature. Shakespeare, of course, had to write
under the particular historical circumstances which existed
at his time; but nevertheless he did put forward general
principles, or universal forms, which he filled with
historical content. Our images of history may have changed,
but the forms remain, and they do not depend upon their
historical content for their artistic validity.

There are dramatic oppositions within Shakespeare as in
any great playwright – between free will and determinism,
between nobility of will, nobility of title and nobility of
deed, between appearance and reality, between men and
women, between classes. It's possible to argue that a play,
say, like *Cymbeline* suggests that it is the outcasts, the

141

supposedly low-born, who will actually provide the salvation that society needs. In a play like *The Winter's Tale*, it's possible to regard Perdita as a vindication of the fact that nobility of title doesn't necessarily mean nobility of thought and deed. These are matters of interpretation.

A look at *Othello* illustrates the tendency to regard Shakespeare's plays purely in terms of their particular historical origins and not in terms of the general and symbolic meaning that they might possess. Shakespeare gives Othello lines like: 'Her name, that was as fresh as Dian's visage, is now begrim'd and black as mine own face' or, 'O yet mortal engines, whose rude throats th'immortal Jove's dread clamours counterfeit.' He says to Amelia, 'You, mistress, have had the office opposite to St Peter.' And so forth. We have a portrait of a Moor talking not in the language of his putative Islamic origins, but in Christian and classical terms, such as Dian, Jove, St Peter and Patience, 'thou Rose of a Cherubim'.

Now: is this a portrait of a man who is an apostate, who has been cut adrift from his ethnic, religious and cultural moorings, so to speak? Or is it a portrait of a man who is truly liberated in that he can use the words of an imperialist culture, the only language that his listeners will understand, and does so, cynically and deliberately, in much the same way as a modern black American might say, 'Nigger, you so bad, you beautiful.'

Or is it possible that Shakespeare simply got it wrong, that he'd never met a Moor in his life, and he was simply using a convenient literary and dramatic stereotype for dramatic expediency and effect? I say again, this is all a matter of interpretation.

What is lamentable is when interpretation becomes a matter of tradition, and so, instead of asking these questions or taking a line on this particular point of the play, we have a tedious, irrelevant and to my mind offensive debate as to whether Shakespeare intended Othello to be a Moor or a veritable negro. And the implication here is that if he were a Moor, he'd be a civilized man, closer to the European style, a civilized man tricked into savage excesses. If he were a veritable negro, he'd be in essence a savage with only a veneer of civilization.

That kind of debate misses the point entirely; and our problem is how to shake free from a particular historical tradition which has led us to interpret Shakespeare in certain ways, and particularly has led us to believe that Shakespeare can only be understood in the light of the historical conditions that existed at the time he wrote.

Ian Herbert thanked Hugh Quarshie for providing a bridge from the discussion about the Englishness of Shakespeare to his supposed feudal longings; and he invited Ernst Schumacher to tread a little further along that bridge.

ERNST SCHUMACHER: I guess my English is very bad and I prefer to have the support of a long, long text. I am a professor! But I would like now merely to try for a few small points of my own. Is Shakespeare a feudal propagandist? Naturally, I think that he was a propagandist of the feudal system. He came from the gentry and he had to have the protection of the court. He had to have the help of noblemen, but he also realized that the court was only part of society as a whole, within the people, under the people. I speak as a Marxist, this being in the language of the Bible. He was naturally a contemporary of his time, but he has remained a man for all times.

Obviously, I can't talk now about all the plays, but will have to confine my attention to one or two of them. Let's look at the past, and recent, history of *The Merchant of Venice*. Shakespeare wrote this play in connection with an alleged criminal, political criminal, conspiracy of a Jewish physician in (I think) 1593. He was decapitated and he was used by the aristocracy to inflame hatred against the Jewish people. And two very well-known plays came from that event, Marlowe's *The Jew of Malta* and Shakespeare's play. In Germany, *The Merchant of Venice* has always played a very bad role in the sentiments against the Jewish people. It was revived and played in Berlin at the beginning of the nineteenth century, and of course, in the twentieth century, to inflame hatred against the Jews. Hitler used it, Goebbels used it, and it contributed directly to the extermination of the Jews, the 'final solution' of 1943. The Minister for Propaganda is quoted in the six files for the extermination of the Jewish people as ordering a performance of *The Merchant of Venice*. And where was this production played? Where was the performance? In a courtyard in Vienna, because Hitler was originally inspired by the forces of antisemitism in Austria. Werner Kraus, a very well-known actor in Germany at the time, who often appeared in propaganda films to ridicule the Jew, was selected personally by Goebbels to play in *The Merchant of Venice* and critics wrote about his performance as Shylock that 'this is a warped picture of the Eastern Jews, a sub-human man'. The character was clear, he was there to help people to realize that such objects must be exterminated. It was a typical use of Shakespeare in a false way to justify the 'final solution' of the Jewish question. It is impossible in my view to play *The Merchant of Venice* in Germany after this example.

Such usages of Shakespeare make me sceptical about all such interpretations of Shakespeare. At the beginning of the 1920s, after the October Revolution, and the development of the workers' movement and the creation of left-wing theatre, we started to think about Shakespeare in a different way. Was he a feudal propagandist? It was a thought which linked writers and theatre makers in Berlin, the Soviet Union and in Britain. The attacks on Shakespeare began with the idea that 'Shakespeare is the mouthpiece for a very frightened personality'. They were based on the conviction that the great men in his society, the noblemen, were only great because they were standing on mountains of corpses. And where in Shakespeare is the recognition of that fact? Where are the people? Where are the victims of great men? And that led on to the question, what should we do about Shakespeare?

It was a question posed and considered naturally and intensively by Brecht. In his first period, he thought it was possible to play Shakespeare in a favourable light, by indicating that one side of the Shakespearian heroes and their destinies are fused with those of their victims; but later on, he felt that this was not good enough, not clear enough. If you take the example of *Coriolanus*, he disliked the treatment of the people by Shakespeare, and the respect for Coriolanus, a very, very weak man. And so he changed the play to make the proletariat speak more simply and naturally, like Bolshevik communists. It was not very convincing. Much more convincing is the change at the end of *Coriolanus*, where he is given the information that the people of Rome are against him.

Brecht had a slogan: Shakespeare changes, only if we can change Shakespeare. It is a symbolic answer. It is very, very difficult to eliminate the extreme feudal points of view in Shakespeare and substitute the democratic views. And yet the older I grow, the more I distrust the judgement of my rational, my materialistic, my Marxist mind which believes in a positive Utopia. The older I grow, the more I believe that the pre-Marxist Brecht was all right, at least he was right for the 1920s.

There is nothing more stupid than to perform Shakespeare in such a way that he is clear. He is unclear by nature. He is pure matter. But if there has ever been a play by Shakespeare which has stayed true for all time, and demonstrates that Shakespeare is our contemporary, and where it is high time that this clarity be recognized as a historical truth, it is his insight into the viciousness of man in *Troilus and Cressida*: 'Lechery, lechery: still, wars and lechery. Nothing else holds fashion. A burning devil take them.'

'It's remarkable', commented Ian Herbert, 'to hear a Marxist and a Brechtian scholar suggesting that the pre-Marxist Brecht may have made one or two good points! Michael Handelsaltz told me yesterday that the most performed Shakespearian play in Israel is in fact *The Merchant of Venice*!' He then introduced Richard Wilson from Lancaster University, the author of the Penguin Masters Series edition of *Julius Caesar*, who was in the process of completing a book on Shakespeare and Carnival.

RICHARD WILSON: Far from being a feudal propagandist, Shakespeare, as we have just seen, is our contemporary in alarming ways.

Citing Cramner's prophecy over the infant Elizabeth, in *Henry VIII*, one of Britain's most renowned Shakespeare commentators, the critic G.Wilson Knight, was able to find there a detailed prediction and total justification of Mrs Thatcher's Falklands policy. Interviewed on his views about the Task Force in the middle of the campaign, Wilson

Knight replied, 'Our key must be Cranmer's royal prophecy.'

'This I still hold to be our one authoritative statement,' Wilson Knight said, 'every word deeply significant as forecast of the world order at which we aim. It involves not just democracy, but democracy in strict subservience to the Crown. It follows that I support Mrs Thatcher and our activities, now or in the future, in so far as they may be expanding British tradition and our national heritage to world proportions.'

Well, Wilson Knight was an old man in 1982 and past his most persuasive, but his concept of Shakespeare as our contemporary and a kind of guardian angel or unpaid consultant to Mrs Thatcher's war cabinet is not quite as eccentric as it sounds. In particular, Wilson Knight's belief that Shakespeare's meaning is bound up with his forecast of 'democracy in strict subservience' to order or the status quo is one which is continually being reproduced in exam papers, newspapers, programme notes, and wherever Shakespeare is recycled for relevance to society today.

For example, when the Young Vic began a series of radical re-interpretations of the plays in 1984, the critics savaged the approach as 'Spart-ish tosh'; complaining that David Thacker was 'tying the texts' in what one called 'a political strait-jacket', 'which in effect dares to tell Shakespeare what he was writing about'. The productions were dismissed as 'well-staged but wrong-headed', since it was nothing less than an 'atrocity' to expose the impressionable young to such 'unashamedly political left-wing comic strip simplifications'. 'Is the theatre the place', one critic demanded,' for political statements?'

Yet a few hundred yards away on the South Bank, the National Theatre's *Coriolanus* was being hailed in some cases by the self-same critics as 'a triumph', precisely because, it seemed, its director, Peter Hall, had realized Shakespeare's 'burning political relevance'. What this meant was spelt out in *The Daily Telegraph*, where Hall was praised for a staging that 'transcends logic to underline the political topicality of a play about the threat to democracy when workers are misled by troublemakers'.

Coriolanus, the critics agreed, was 'a piece for Britain in the 1980s', and Hall was congratulated for a 'totally political reading of the play', in which 'the affairs of the nation are aired with maximum fairness to all sides'. As Michael Billington enthused in *The Guardian*, 'What makes this a great production is that it connects directly with modern Britain to show conviction government and popular anarchy in headlong, nightmare collision.' In the year of the miners' strike, it appeared that what Billington had called the 'message of *Coriolanus*' was that 'good government depends upon compromise'. 'This is the best Shakespeare production to emerge from the National in its twenty-one years!' exclaimed Billington. 'And the reason is not far to seek. Abandoning the academic approach, Hall champions the radical middle. This *Coriolanus* belongs as much to the SDP as the SPQR.' So: 'academic' considerations, and even 'logic', were discarded in the case of a Shakespeare production that worked in the correct political interests. Nor was there any question now of the director presuming to tell Shakespeare what he was writing about. A really magnificent production of this great play, we were led to believe, was one that quite literally endorsed the policies of David Owen.

The charm of newspaper criticism is that it betrays its ideology so blatantly. While Shakespeare's plays are packaged in this way, they typify the process by which the classic text is reproduced in our society to authorize the moral claims of market capitalism. Here the confusion of maximum fairness to all sides with the aims of the managerial class is comically naive. But the same identification of the affairs of the nation with the priorities of its business classes has been the hall-mark, and arguably the function, of the British Shakespeare Industry since the First World War.

When Sam Wanamaker's Globe Theatre Trust faced a sceptical Southwark public recently, the bard was represented on the platform by a company chairman, the leader of the Liberal peers, an RSC actor and a local Alliance MP, while the police and property developers hovered visibly in the wings. Afterwards the actor-son of the Attorney-General complained that Sam's opponents on Southwark Labour Council had 'made Shakespeare political'. He could presumably see no politics in Simon Hughes', the Alliance MP's, claim that the Globe had been 'a people's theatre', where the very shape of the building had united everyone and would do so again, if the Alliance has its way. The reason he could not read this as a political statement is that the idea of the Globe as a democratic forum, and of Shakespeare as the prophet of democracy, in strict subservience to order, is so taken for granted. In fact, the myth of the democratic Globe dates from the great panic following the European revolutions of 1917–20, and was created by critics such as F.R. Leavis, who idealized Elizabethan England as a classless, organic community whose 'people talked, so making Shakespeare possible'.

It was a legend that received definitive shape during the Second World War, when the American scholar Alfred Harbage described the Globe as 'the cradle of Anglo-Saxon democracy'. 'The theatre of a nation for which the only price of admission', he said, 'was the possession by each spectator of some spiritual vitality.' With its lords and groundlings, this is the concept of the Elizabethan theatre that has become fixed in our schools in a thousand *papier mâché* replicas. And though, as research now shows, it ignores the non-playgoing 80 per cent of London's population, and though it grossly distorts the middle-class character of the Globe's audience, it is an image which remains essential to the status of Shakespeare as the 'National Poet', who, because he is assumed to have appealed to all classes, wrote for 'democracy' and 'not for an age, but for all time'.

On the only occasion when a poll was taken of Shakespeare's audience, when the police raided the Globe in 1602, the theatre was 'full of lawyers and their clerks, country gentlemen that had law-suits, knights; the Queen's men and even earls'. The theatre, incidentally, was closed on the only day – Sunday – when working men regularly were free from work. Small surprise then that modern critics find a message in the plays that has to do with what happens 'when workers are misled by troublemakers'.

Shakespeare was no feudalist. The very act of putting on stage the uncrowning or assassination of a monarch struck an intellectual blow at the ailing heart of England's feudal system, which is why the deposition scene of *Richard II* was banned until the eighteenth century. As we've been told so often, these plays are concerned with 'things dying' and 'things new-born', an old order giving way to a new. But Shakespeare's preference for a new order is not necessarily any longer ours.

Since this discussion raises the question, it might be as well to try to define the social and economic order which Shakespeare seems aptly to have in mind in the resolutions of his plays. Put crudely, these dramas are about the need to reconcile individual competitive drives, sexual drives towards free choice in love, for instance, as well as the proprietorial and materialistic drives that Michael Bogdanov has described, the need to harness these drives to the purposes of a hierarchic state. They dramatize the dangers to order and the status quo of individualism and materialism; and they seem to reach towards a new world where these forces are realized 'in strict subservience' – to use Wilson Knight's phrase – 'to a unified state'. This is a vision which is practically a blueprint for the early stage of market capitalism known as mercantilism, in which market forces were made to serve the national interest and the thrusting new energies of business were accommodated with the archaic forms of the feudal state – monarchy, aristocracy and inherited wealth. Mercantilism came early in Britain and struck deep.

If we continue to discover meaning in these plays that seem to be models of such a compromise, it may be because English society has changed so little in its antiquated class system. I would argue that Shakespeare is, if anything, actually a propagandist of mercantilism, who seeks a reconciliation between social order and economic freedom, and a very English compromise between the private need to make money or make love and the public need to recognize limits laid down from above.

As it happens, everything we know about 'the man Shakespeare' confirms the bias of his plays. It's simply not true that we know nothing about Shakespeare. In fact, we know far more about him than most other Elizabethan individuals and, as collected by Stanley Schoenbaum, the documents detailing his life – deeds, testaments, receipts, law records, wills, leases, and so on – fill a very substantial book. It's just that critics turn their noses up at this bourgeois life-style and prefer to ignore it. Whether dealing in textiles at markets in the Midlands, making a profit on grain in a famine year, or colluding with the enclosure of the commons around Stratford, Shakespeare the man was typical of the seventeenth-century gentry and business families, the groups who overthrew the king, not to upset the whole applecart but, in Christopher Hill's words, 'to make the world safe to make profits in'. There *is* a new world coming in Shakespearian drama, but we must not make the mistake of believing that the order towards which the plays move is a timeless and universal one.

That, unfortunately, was the implication of the book whose publication we are celebrating at this conference. Jan Kott's description of what he terms 'the grand mechanism of history in Shakespeare' overthrew the wartime picture, enshrined in films like Olivier's *Henry V*. But it must be said that Kott's alternative picture of a Shakespearian world which was like our world because, as he said, 'it did not regain its balance after the earthquake' was also, by implication, deeply conservative. Its view of human behaviour, as revealed through the plays as essentially and unchangingly animal-like and its constant reference to the absurdism of Beckett belong to the last days of modernism and the post-war recoil from politics. But in its insistence that Shakespeare's world is ours, that 'the implacable roller of history crushes everybody and everything' and that the human condition is forever the same and forever hopeless, *Shakespeare Our Contemporary* offers no possibility of change and no analysis of failure. Anguish at the world of Auschwitz and Hiroshima produces only a paralysed acquiescence in the belief that this is simply and for all time 'the way things are' and that to contest them is futile, because Shakespeare shows us that this is what it means and always has meant to be human.

'There is no document of civilization', wrote the German critic Walter Benjamin, 'that is not also a document of barbarism.' What he meant was that the very conditions that produce literature are founded on exploitation. In Shakespeare's case, it would be a very naive director or teacher who denied that, yes, 'the dyers' hands' are the deepest red, with stains of exploitation. In terms of property, class, nationality, sexuality, and race, the Warwickshire landowner and textile speculator voices the world view of an enlightened, but none the less determined, middle class. Its 'new world' will be born if necessary (and in Shakespeare's favourite image) by the force of Caesarian section. Rising then, this is the middle class that has since ruled England by keeping 'democracy subservient'.

Criticism must not mistake its view of human nature as the God-given truth about men and women, but equally the inheritance of Shakespeare and the bourgeois culture he represents is simply too heavy to be thrown off or discarded, the pleasure that has been created through the plays too powerful to be refused. As Martin Esslin said, 'Shakespeare is the form in which our national mythology has been concentrated.' But, as Brecht pointed out, there is no reason why that mythology must always mean the same to succeeding generations. The function of criticism today must be, on the contrary, to analyse the ways in which meaning has been produced for different social and political purposes in Shakespeare's texts – and the ways in which the texts are reproduced today in schools, theatres, newspapers, and Parliament.

'*Coriolanus*', declared Nigel Lawson recently in an interview, 'is written from the Tory point of view. It says that man doesn't change, or man's nature doesn't change. The same problems are there in different forms: the fact of difference and the need for hierarchy. Both these facts are expressed', the Chancellor claimed, 'more powerfully by Shakespeare than anybody, the fact of difference and the need for hierarchy. Shakespeare was a Tory without any doubt.'

Lawson here demonstrates the oppressive, conservative weight of the idea that Shakespeare is 'our contemporary'.

But there is quite literally too much capital invested here, for radicals to throw away. Shakespeare is too valuable to British society to be disposed of like the family silver. As an art object, a monument to the old gods, Shakespearian drama must be re-interpreted, re-deployed, re-occupied. In the work of directors such as David Thacker and Michael Bogdanov, Shakespeare may yet prove the Trojan horse to storm the cultural citadel.

Ian Herbert then introduced Erich Fried, who began by apparently agreeing with Richard Wilson.

ERICH FRIED: Any attempt to try and understand Shakespeare not as a man of his time is doomed to failure and misrepresentation. Karl Marx, who was a profound admirer of Shakespeare, knew this very well. Shakespeare, of course, was no fighter. He would have been killed very quickly if, in his time, he had been a fighter. But he was beautifully subversive; and his psychological insight and his sensuality, his observation of human beings and of the world, helped him in this. He shows Henry IV as a weak, paranoic murderer, struck by pangs of conscience but not changing his life according to that conscience. He shows that the victory of Henry IV, the king's cause over the rebels, was due to foul treachery. He shows that the glorious fight of Henry V in France is a war of aggression without any good foundation. It was prepared towards the end of *Henry IV* in order to divert the attention of powerful people in the country from upsetting the English state, and is shown at the beginning of *Heny V* in the miserable tirades of some priests who are trying to make out a case against France. He shows how the famous hero Achilles slays Hector in the most cowardly and treacherous manner. And he certainly wasn't a defender of democracy.

Democracy wasn't even born in his time, and we know that democracy isn't born in our time either, although we choose to think otherwise. But, of course, he did show up the injustices, the miseries – how the acts of the great, the so-called great, whom he unmasks, are reflected in the suffering and corruption of small people. He does that all the time. His span, his greatness as a dramatist, his ability to encompass the horrors, was based in the experience of his time. Of course, *The Merchant of Venice* is always used by some commentators to further racist intolerance, even if the actors do not intend it that way. But Shakespeare, while giving the people their nasty Jew, equips Shylock with a psychological depth which none of the other characters have, and chooses to demonstrate that the trial is an absolutely merciless and shameless parody of justice by a fake lawyer, in which the woman then in the end by a trick wreaks vengeance on Antonio, who has loved her husband. Hans Meyer, the German literary critic, has described very clearly how the outsider, Antonio, is homo-erotically tied to this woman's man, and how Shakespeare with just a few strokes of the pen manages to sketch in that remarkable insight.

It is very important not to underrate what Shakespeare did in his time. The cruelty and span of human possibilities, of inhuman possibilities, from *Titus Andronicus* to *Othello*, are necessary, if we are not to have a drama of people who are smaller than life. His characters are not larger than life, but they are life without taboos, life without censorship, without pulling punches.

In Germany, it's comparatively easy to bring out the barbarisms, not because they have a stronger stomach for them, but because in their recent history they've had a ring-side seat to watch similar ones. In England, it's different. Although the German Establishment are almost as bad lick-spittles to the Americans nowadays as the English Establish-ment, they have had a tradition of revolt in Germany, dating back to the students' revolt and extending even to terror-ism. In England, there is nothing like that. English papers, like *The Guardian*, in a civilized way make fun, but half secretly, of a creep like Reagan, so that an ordinary reader couldn't even understand it, if he isn't well informed. But they describe none the less events which ought to make the blood of every person who still has blood in his veins, boil. But they describe them as if they were nice.

I have just read a story in *The Observer* about people in an English village, where Indians who were not let into the country are marooned; and the bastards in that village

153

would be capable of erecting a gas chamber, or at least applaud the erection of a gas chamber, if they are too cowardly to do it themselves. But the story is presented as if it were a politely funny story, and I think this is despicable. I think that in a way the English today are in a very sad phase of their history where one could almost say that they are not worthy of Shakespeare any more.

But Shakespeare, of course, has in his plays the substance so that a decent performance can recreate the feelings to make the people worthy of Shakespeare again. One mustn't make the mistake of thinking of one main characteristic or quality in Shakespeare. Mao Tse-Tung spoke of the main contradiction, and of the main enemy, and I at the time tried to make fun of it, by saying *vis à vis* my fight against the main enemy, 'I was killed by my secondary enemy.' In trying to fight, to show up something in order to fight against alienation, against self-alienation, against vilification, against lack of feeling and insensibility, it is no good just to *want* to do it. One must also have it inside oneself, otherwise it becomes top-heavy; and Shakespeare was able at the same time to show the greatest horrors and, in between, to be funny and show love, and all kinds of things.

It is wrong, for example, in *Troilus and Cressida* for Cressida to be played from the start as a kind of prostitute. She's just weak and gets ground down by society. At the beginning she's almost a Juliet. And Ophelia is not a person who is just a court creature, but she is a court creature and a human being who is in danger of being destroyed in the process as well. It is important to recognize that Shakespeare's sensitivity and span was such that he didn't deny the possibilities of barbarism in society and in himself, in his attitudes to things, and that he was able to describe barbarism in a non-hypocritical manner.

The way to rescue Shakespeare is, of course, in the long run the way to try to rescue the world and our society. You cannot have justice in an unjust society and you cannot have great drama in the long run in a rotten society.

'David Hare', said Ian Herbert, 'has written several plays about the rottenness in our society. He is now directing Shakespeare's supreme indictment of the rottenness of his society, *King Lear.*'

DAVID HARE: There is a bewildering variety of interpretations for all of Shakespeare's plays. He shares with Jesus Christ and Karl Marx the ability to be interpreted all ways by true believers who believe that they alone have some understanding and that elsewhere he is completely misrepresented. *King Lear*, for example, is currently on the course at the Harvard Business School where it's studied as an exercise in bad delegation!

The only place where Shakespeare can really be understood is in the theatre and that's why I find talking about him rather difficult. And I also find frankly that in rehearsing Shakespeare what a critic can offer is of very limited value. To take an example: the justice's scene in *King Lear*, where Lear tries the stools, claiming them or believing them to be his daughters. In the Arden Edition, there are barely two lines at the top of the page, and virtually a whole page of interpretation underneath. You have to turn through about thirty pages to get through the scene; and when you sit around a table and try to work out what the lines mean, it's almost impossible to make sense of them! But the minute you begin to play them, then the sense becomes blindingly clear.

I find this deeply mysterious. If you come from the tradition of theatre that I come from, from the Royal Court Theatre and the English rational tradition, the first thing you try to do is to find out the sense of what the text means, what it is actually saying. And having discovered that, you put it into practice. But the art of acting Shakespeare is organically different. In the act of finding the emotion behind the line, finding the feeling behind the line, you start to sense what the meaning of the line is; and in *King Lear*, much of the text is so obscure or corrupt that it's almost impossible to find out what certain words do mean.

The only critic I've read who has something interesting to say, although I don't agree with it, is Middleton Murry. He wrote: 'I'm something of a heretic with regard to *King Lear*. It seems to me definitely inferior to the other great tragedies of Shakespeare. I would almost believe that Shakespeare was on the verge of madness himself when he wrote *King Lear*. *Hamlet*, *Othello* and *Macbeth* are tragedies, but they are evidence of entire imaginative mastery in their author. But in *King Lear*, I find disturbance, hesitation, uncertainty, and a constant interruption of the predominant passion.

'It is one of the things which has become by convention impossible to say, but *King Lear* makes upon me the impression of the work of a Shakespeare who is out of his depth. He does not know really what he wants to say. Perhaps he does not know whether he wants to say anything: "An ounce of civet, good apothecary, to sweeten my imagination!" is to my ear the voice of a man through whom *King Lear* was uttered. And there is a vital difference between such possession and the spontaneous self-abeyance which is the attitude of imagination. A man imagines with his whole being. A man possessed as Shakespeare may have been possessed during the writing of *King Lear* by the vision that is continually breaking forth in it, cannot imagine with his whole being. To use such terms as these *King Lear* impresses me as a constant struggle of imagination against possession – a struggle in which in the main the imagination is defeated.'

This seems to me the basic complaint made by critics against Shakespeare – that what he says can't be reduced to a few sentences, to tenets. Because critics themselves want to organize the world into a neat column that runs down a newspaper or can be turned through the pages of a book, they imagine that an investigatory writer, who writes in order to find out what he believes, and not because he already believes something and sets out a play to demonstrate a diagram of what he believes, must be 'possessed'. Middleton Murry calls him 'possessed' because he's in the act of finding out what he believes even as he writes, and the immediacy of Shakespeare's writing comes from the fact that he is discovering in the process of writing. Of course, in that there is contradiction, but that is not his weakness as a writer but the essence of his greatness as a writer – that he discovers what he believes as he goes along.

Do I mean therefore something as naive as this, that Shakespeare doesn't know what he thinks? Well, if we say that he doesn't know the answers in *King Lear* when he sets himself the questions of life and death themselves, that he's out of his depth, we're saying nothing at all. We're all out of our depths when facing those questions; but Shakespeare comes closer to confronting them than any man who's lived.

I deduce a few political views from his work, no more than a political axis. You can say of him that plainly he isn't an anarchist. He does believe in power, he believes that power is necessary in society, he believes that the giving away of your kingdom is a fundamentally foolish act, and to give away power without making any real provision for the transfer of that power is a wrong thing to do. He believes that power must be vested somewhere in a society, it must be organized in some way, and he believes that if you throw power away, worse things may follow.

But he also believes, and this is what makes the plays so intriguing, that anyone who believes that his power is real, will come to a terrible end. That is the balance, that you must simultaneously behave as if power exists – and yet you mustn't behave as if that power is real. If you come to believe that your power is real, if you come to believe in the judge's cloak and the king's crown, then you will come to a terrible end.

The way to wisdom in *King Lear* is represented through madness, what Edgar calls 'reason and impertinency mixed'.

The scenes of the fourth act are very close to what Christ offered in the Sermon on the Mount, with the propositions that to be wise one must first be foolish, to be rich you must first be poor, to be sane you must first of all be mad.

These propositions are so radical, so overwhelming, that I don't think that anybody has ever begun to grasp their meaning and very few have tried to live them; but you can feel the whole weight of Shakespeare's imaginative genius when he starts to describe what these radical propositions are.

Ian Herbert then asked Alexander Anikst whether these views seemed so radical in the Soviet Union.

ALEXANDER ANIKST: First of all, I should say that in a way I am more responsible for today's discussion than anyone else here, because it all started with the trouble made by Karl

Marx – and I am a Marxist. I belong to the first country in the world which made Marxism a state ideology; and the problem of Shakespeare has a history in our life. And I am old enough to have gone through almost all the stages of Shakespearian sociological criticism in the Soviet Union.

We were the first to adopt the view that art and literature reflect life struggles in society; and it's very important that all these discussions always refer to present-day ideological and social struggles. Marxist criticism in our country started at a period when class struggle there was very strong, shortly after the civil war, when Russia underwent a complete transformation. Class conflicts were very strong in our country and the first Soviet approach to literature and art was to apply the principle of class struggle to this field as well.

Of course, Shakespeare was always a very important factor in the social and cultural life of Russia, and the first sociological Marxist treatment of Shakespeare came to this – that Shakespeare was a representative of aristocracy, of feudalism; because the subject matter of his plays is for the most part feudal society, his heroes belong to the feudal classes. Such was the view proposed by the first Marxist critics, but then people remembered that, after all, Shakespeare's art was that of a certain epoch, of the Renaissance, and the Renaissance was the period of the rising bourgeoisie.

And so other critics came along, Professor Alexander Smirnoff, who said that Shakespeare was a typical representative of the Renaissance, a writer of the rising humanist bourgeoisie, who had good reason to support him because there is no doubt of humanist ideology in Shakespeare. It is there in all his works. But then a third reaction came, from the Hungarian critic who lived in Moscow, Georg Lukács, who came forth with the idea that great art cannot be given over to the exploiting classes, that Shakespeare was neither feudal nor bourgeois. We borrowed the German idea of 'folk quality', 'folk popularity'; and as a result, there came a group of critics who proposed the view that Shakespeare is to be taken as a representative of folk art, popular theatre, popular drama. He is not the spokesman of any one social class.

Those who have primitive ideas of Marxism think that Marxists divide everything into classes and do not except any variations, which is entirely wrong. Marx and Engels in particular believed that the problems of ideology are very complicated and that there are many variations in the field of ideology. There is one passage in Engels' work, *The Peasant War in Germany*, where he speaks about one man who was very active then called Thomas Müntzer, who was a cleric and by birth and education a member of the bourgeoisie, but whose views and actions could speak for a cross-section of all society. Marxism does not believe that the social position of man is the decisive factor. History proves that this is not so. Karl Marx himself was a bourgeois by origin but not a bourgeois by ideology. Lenin also came from the ruling classes, but was not an ideologue of the ruling classes. So in social life, things happen which enable us to approach Shakespeare from a very wide point of view historically. Historically, his position as a popular dramatist means that to call him a feudal propagandist would be wrong – but to say the opposite would also be wrong. Why? Because social analysis demands a very thorough understanding of the period. Shakespeare's time was a period of transition, of changing. If you speak of aristocracy of that time, first of all you cannot speak of real feudal aristocracy, because all the feudal aristocracy was killed in the Wars of the Roses. There was a new gentry, more bourgeois in their habits, though they retained all the feudal privileges. It was a new kind of class formation and so it was natural that these new men, many of them, adopted humanist ideology. People like Philip Sidney. To speak of him as a representative of a modern feudal class would be entirely wrong, because the most important thing about him was that he had adopted the humanist views.

Shakespeare was a representative of the cross-section of English society that was present in his theatre. You had there all the classes of British society and Shakespeare was a man who adapted his art in such a way that the audience of Shakespeare's theatre felt quite at home. I quite agree with Richard Wilson who said that it would be nonsense to speak of Shakespeare's democracy. The time wasn't then right for democracy. Shakespeare could mock at the simple folk, at the pit, and nobody would take offence, because the idea of democracy had not risen in society. Although Shakespeare evidently felt sympathy for the poor and the naked, he did not have the least idea of them getting the upper hand in society and having the power in their hands. Shakespeare was too practical a man to quarrel with authorities.

This happens in every theatre in every age. I don't believe that the National Theatre can stage a communist play, though I believe that the people at the National Theatre are very progressive in mind and are humanistic in their attitude towards life. But there are circumstances which you cannot jump over. Shakespeare never did jump over them in his time. His plays do not oppose the existing order. No, he was *for* order. But what is interesting is that his idea of order was so central to social well-being that all the plays of Shakespeare show that order breaks up. Order is always being destroyed, until that point where it has to be re-established.

Shakespeare was a genius because he felt that the main thing in the life of his time was this constant attempt to destroy the existing order, to go against it, because of the birth of individualism, of the birth of the first elements of bourgeois society, of everything that showed that the old order is dying out. Something new is being born and Shakespeare's playwriting is the best mirror of his time because it shows that that is what is happening.

When we ask 'Where were Shakespeare's sympathies? With the old or with the new?' then there is a variety of answers. In Shakespeare you will find a sympathy with people who do not belong to this order of things, who are newcomers but good people – Othello, for example – and at the same time he will show you newcomers who are bad people – Iago. They both belong to the period of social change, but some are good and some are bad. You can say of Hotspur that he is a typical feudal knight, but there is something about him which makes you sympathetic for him. He's very human, his energy, his pride, it's not feudal but human. Shakespeare's people do not belong to this class or that class, purely and simply. His people all belong to changing times. They're in *King Lear*, the old feudal servants and the new individuals. That is the source of Shakespeare's greatness. It was due to his time, of course, to the period. There are times which are favourable for great art and for certain types of persons.

We know that there have been only two great periods of tragedy, ancient Greece and Elizabethan England, both periods of great change. History helped the ancient playwrights, history helped Shakespeare and his contemporaries. You have to take a broad, historical view of Shakespeare in order to see that the greatness of Shakespeare's mind could grasp the contradictions of his period, which is why his plays are also full of contradictions with characters who have the conflicts of their times born into their souls. That is why Shakespeare is the greatest dramatist in the world.

'Ruby Cohn has asked to speak last', said Ian Herbert, 'because she wants to talk not about Shakespeare as a propagandist, but of Shakespeare used for propaganda purposes.' Ruby Cohn, a Professor of Comparative Drama at the University of California, is a theatre critic, author and editor of many collections of critical essays, including, in 1976, *Modern Shakespeare Offshoots*.

RUBY COHN: Not quite propaganda purposes perhaps, but you can make your own definition. I would like to draw your attention to some British playwrights – and the uses they have made of Shakespeare in their plays. But I'm not going to speak of what is probably the best-known play derived from Shakespeare, Tom Stoppard's *Rosencrantz and Guildenstern are Dead*, because it doesn't come within the scope of this discussion. In the play, he evades the question of politics almost entirely by setting the play on a quasi-metaphysical plane.

The playwrights I want to talk about are all left-wing; and obliquely all four call Shakespeare to task for being something like a feudal propagandist. They therefore adapt certain Shakespeare plays to make them more relevant to the particular situation of what they feel is still unfortunately this sceptred isle. These four playwrights are Edward Bond, David Hare, David Edgar and Howard

161

Brenton. All have been fairly candid about their politics. Bond and Brenton in particular have had some very unflattering things to say about Shakespeare in their interviews and prefaces. Brenton has been quoted as being 'impatient of all this Shakespeare shit'. But they return to that shit to convert it into their own plays.

I'll start with Bond, because he's a decade older than the others, and has been most consistently haunted by Shakespeare in what Martin Esslin called a 'Shakespeare trilogy'. He wrote his own *Lear* which takes Shakespeare to task for creating a feudal monarch. Bond's Lear has only two daughters, Goneril and Regan, and those two daughters remain as evil in Bond's play as in Shakespeare's; but there is a revolution against Bond's Lear led, eventually, by Cordelia. Cordelia becomes dictator of the kingdom and she has learnt nothing from Lear's suffering.

Lear tries to persuade her unsuccessfully of a kind of democracy; and though old and blind at the end of the play, he climbs up to the wall that he himself originally constructed to defend his kingdom; and starts to de-construct it, if you will forgive the pun. He gets shot for doing so. But he has learnt. He is a more explicitly socially redeemed Lear than Shakespeare with all his ambiguities, chose to portray.

A few years later, Bond set Shakespeare on stage in *Bingo*, a very unflattering portrait, even when played by John Gielgud; and a few months after that, Bond based his *The Sea* very obliquely on Shakespeare's *Tempest*. *The Sea* begins with a tempest, ends with a young couple leaving the ancestral home of at least one of them to start a new society – which is roughly how we have in school so often summarized *The Tempest*. In these three plays, Bond seems to have moved from the condemnation of a feudal monarch, as portrayed in *Lear*, to an acceptance of traditional comic resolution. *The Sea* seems to me to be Bond's least angry play, his nearest approach to a comedy.

David Hare doesn't fit so well into my scheme, but I'm not going to let him off for that reason. In *Slag*, he starts with a somewhat similar premise to that of *Love's Labour's Lost*, but instead of having three young men dedicated to the bachelor life, he has three young women wishing to live

162

in a man-free world, and they start a private school for girls which will have nothing to do with men. The parents don't like this idea very much – very rich parents, it's assumed – and gradually all the students withdraw from the school. The three women, as obnoxious a trio as you'd ever want to see on stage, are riddled with fantasies about a man-free world; and by the end of the play, all the fantasies are exploded, and they announce their intention to start another girls' school.

What I think Hare is saying is that, well, perhaps in the renaissance of the feudal structure, everything comes out right in the end – boy gets girl and a new society is founded and the race continues – but there are problems with that facile solution in today's world and the rising tide of feminism cannot be so easily quelled. And he leaves the play with an open question.

David Edgar deals more directly with this panel's theme. His adaptation of *Romeo and Juliet* is called *Death Story*, the title itself giving some indication of what he does to that tale of deathless love. The beginning is not unlike *Romeo and Juliet*, the critical difference being that Juliet belongs to the Capulets who are the capitalists of Verona, and Romeo belongs to the Montagu family, who are expert craftsmen beginning to recognize their power by organizing trade unions. This play places the class conflict at the centre of *Romeo and Juliet*.

The friar, or priest in Edgar's play, has much the same notion as to how to bring them together. Juliet will take some drug, look dead and go into hospital, Romeo will visit her there and this beautiful young couple will tear at everybody's heartstrings, the opposing families will relent and everyone will live happily ever after. The only problem with the priest's scheme is that he has evidently told it to other people, so that when Romeo comes to the hospital, he is seized by the thugs who work for the capitalists. Romeo in turn has not trusted the priest, and has come armed to the hospital, so that, like the hero of a grade B movie, he shoots his way out of the trap and without so much as a backward glance at Juliet, he goes to join his labouring-class brethren to fight for greater working-class rights. Juliet rehearses various possibilities of suicide but doesn't use any of them, and ends the play with the line, 'How I wish we were dead'.

The question is, who is this 'we'? Romeo and Juliet? Her whole family? The whole capitalist class? But that is left to the audience to determine.

Finally, Howard Brenton, the most vituperative of the four in his horror of the mythic importance of Shakespeare to the British stage, has adapted two of Shakespeare's plays, *Measure for Measure* and *Twelfth Night*, which he calls *Thirteenth Night*. He keeps the title and, by and large, the characters of *Measure for Measure*, but makes Isabel and Claudio black. Isabel is a black bible singer, Claudio a successful rock star. The Duke and Angelo both wish to be dictators of this island kingdom; and are secretly plotting against each other.

There is a Mary Whitehouse kind of movement in Britain, though a bit more extreme, and Claudio is arrested in Piccadilly Circus, despite the protests of his loyal groupies. The Lucio character in Brenton's *Measure for Measure* is by profession a film-maker of blue movies, and so he is set up to make a movie of Angelo and Isabel in bed. But Angelo has his own CIA-type little army – and he actually does have Claudio beheaded. He seizes the incriminating movie, has everybody arrested but the old Duke, who is put in a wheelchair and pushed offstage to write his memoirs, the last refuge for retired politicians.

Nearly a decade later, Brenton wrote *Thirteenth Night*, in which a rising young Labour politician, Jack Beaty, is having an affair, although married to a Labour politician. They go to a meeting and are set upon by fascist thugs, so that Jack Beaty falls unconscious to the ground and the rest of the play is his dream while unconscious.

That dream is basically the plot of *Macbeth* with Jack Beaty as Macbeth betraying old-time Labour politicians. Beaty's opponents, meanwhile, are disporting themselves in Californian swimming pools. At the end of the vision the three witches cackle happily at the bad end of everybody with personal political ambitions; and in the last scene of the play, consciousness returns to Jack Beaty and his lover, and they are given a holiday on the beach as a result of being attacked. The last lines of the play are Beaty: 'Peace is not a personal issue, is it?' and his lover answers 'No'. And then there's a freeze – Beaty is still lame from the beating he's had and his lover is about to fling a stone into the sea from the beach – but there's a freeze instead, which I think we should leave as a kind of ironic symbol, not just of the play but of this summary of these playwrights' contributions.

All four have written plays which show that although they may find Shakespeare irrelevant in some aspects, they are nevertheless indebted to him for much of the material, which demonstrates, for them as for the rest of us, how human beings can act together personally and politically at the same time. If Shakespeare were just a feudal propagandist, would they have bothered?

Ian Herbert invited questions from the audience and a speaker asked: 'When we talk about Shakespeare, do we mean one man or are we describing a canon of work which came from actors and comedians as well over a long period of time? He worked with some very experienced actors. Weren't his plays part of that collaboration?'

RICHARD WILSON: We're talking about the plays which contain the input of the entire company and to which Shakespeare put his name. And not just the company, but also the folk element and other voices, aristocratic as well as popular, that go into the composition of the Shakespearian text.

I think it's very important for us to get away from the idea of one authorial authority, away from the idea that authorship is in some sense the seal of authority – and towards the notion that the Shakespearian text is, first of all, a meeting place, a battleground between different voices; and of course, in the reproduction of a Shakespearian text, the plays can be used for different purposes in different ways.

The critic Terence Hawkes tried to show how a particular *Hamlet* was put together by Dover Wilson because of Dover Wilson's fears in 1917 that the Russian Revolution might be followed by an English revolution. 'Shakespeare' is a series of voices, often in conflict with one another, speaking according to the political imperatives of their times.

'I did not mean subsequent interpretations', replied the questioner, 'I meant in the original creative act. Was Shakespeare simply the man who pulled all the ideas together and took the final decisions that somebody has to make. They may not have been committee decisions exactly, but ones taken by a team of creative people and subsequently endorsed by Shakespeare.'

'I think that's nonsense', said Ian Herbert. 'Actors may work with a dramatist, and give him feedback, but I refuse to accept the idea that Shakespeare was written by the company!'

DAVID HARE: If we rely on *Hamlet* at all, Hamlet does say, 'And let not your clowns speak more than is set down for them', which suggests to me that Shakespeare was pretty concerned to exercise his own authorial control, though I agree that the subsequent business of getting together an authoritative text, years later, involves collusion with others.

I'm sure that if we tried to get hold of early plays by David Hare that have never been printed, we'd have a similar problem; but essentially I think that Shakespeare did try to exercise a firm and rigorous control over his work.

'It's alarming to hear', said a member of the audience, 'how *The Merchant of Venice* was used against the Jews. But do you generally agree with the idea that Shylock is the only person in that play with psychological depth?'

'The scene where Shylock is hoist with his own petard', said Hugh Quarshie, 'is really rather ugly. It is difficult to stage *The Merchant of Venice* without somehow reinforcing the history that led to the persecution of the Jews. I'd like to see a version where Shylock was vindicated, but we'd need David Edgar to do that.'

'Well, of course, there was Arnold Wesker's *The Merchant*', a member of the audience pointed out, 'which tried to do something like that, not entirely successfully. Ruby Cohn forgot *The Merchant*.'

'If we don't believe', another speaker intervened, 'that Shakespeare's plays as a whole are feudal propaganda, couldn't we accept that some of his plays are, and dangerously so? He tries to make an unacceptable system tolerable. Take the example of the servant who protests against the torture of Gloucester in *King Lear*. No servant would dare to do that. Shakespeare is putting forward the idea of a loyal servant serving a good master, suggesting that the system is good, if the people are good within it.'

'Brook cut that scene', commented Ruby Cohn.

'Cutting is an easy way of changing an interpretation, isn't it?' said Ian Herbert.

DAVID HARE: I can't understand people who want to re-write Shakespeare. The only time I've been conscious of re-writing Shakespeare, although I've been corrected today, was with *Pravda*, where Howard Brenton and I took the plot of *Richard III*, or the question that interested us in it, which is why is evil so attractive? That's quite an interesting theme for a modern writer. But for a writer to correct Shakespeare just seems to me absurd. To confront him and take him on and say 'No, you've got this wrong' seems to me fatuous, it's pedagogy, and I think Edward Bond's *Lear* is absurd.

ALEXANDER ANIKST: Very often cutting is not just so that the original meaning persists, or doesn't, as the case may be; but simply to remove that which doesn't interest the director very much.

An actor in the audience objected to the idea that Shakespeare is somehow 'unknowable'. 'He tries so hard to understand what is happening in the world and in human experience. He's determined to capture men's thoughts. I don't think that you can fall into the trap of saying "I don't know quite what he meant, and nobody else does, and therefore I'm entitled to interpret him as I like". It's all too subjective.'

Another member of the audience agreed, and asked about censorship. 'We assume that what he wrote in his plays is what he wanted to write, but there may be a tension in his work between what he wanted to say and what he was permitted to write.'

'We do have a few pages in Shakespeare's handwriting', said Richard Wilson, 'of a composite play, *Sir Thomas More*, which has the Master of the Revels, the government censor, scribbling on it, "Omit this scene entirely! Cut out the insurrections!" '

David Hare was asked what he meant by the struggle between imagination and possession. He answered: 'I was quoting Middleton Murry who made a distinction between those plays where Shakespeare is *in control*, and can exercise his imagination, as opposed to those where he was *possessed*, and not in control. Murry believes that you should be in control of your imagination and he disapproves of not being in control. T.S. Eliot made a similar point about *Hamlet*, which he didn't think was a good play.'

'That tells against Murry and Eliot', said Erich Fried. 'Murry had got hold of an essential point. But he only saw it from his own point of view, which was that he should be in control of his unconscious. Like Eliot, he was frightened of the unconscious.'

Ian Herbert asked whether the panel wanted to make any final points before the close of the session.

ALEXANDER ANIKST: What we have seen today is that there are many approaches to Shakespeare and it is sometimes hard to find the common ground. I would like to say that Shakespeare *was* a feudal propagandist, he was a loyal feudal propagandist, and he was also a propagandist of humanity. We have to preserve him for the future, for he belongs to the heritage of mankind.

ERICH FRIED: I want to warn of two mistakes – that every way of interpreting Shakespeare is equally correct, because they aren't, and that of assuming that Marxism is a doctrine. It isn't and Marx would have laughed at the idea.

SHOULD SHAKESPEARE BE
BURIED OR BORN AGAIN?

For the final session there were no speakers billed in the programme and no background notes with quotations to guide the discussion along particular lines. It was time for the jury to decide, or rather the many different juries, for a feature of the weekend had been the way in which many small groups had gathered together in the Young Vic's coffee bar and in the pubs around Waterloo Road to discuss Shakespeare as if he really were their contemporary.

By now, the formal gap between our invited guests and the public who had bought their tickets had disappeared; and we were all in one room together, the practitioners and the critics, the academics and the students, those with little knowledge of English (but much of Shakespeare) and those with little knowledge of Shakespeare (but much of English), trying to focus our attention on one main question and several subsidiary ones. To what extent is it possible to treat Shakespeare as if he were our contemporary? Are we flattering or abusing his plays by doing so? And what does the world-wide attention to Shakespeare tell us either about him or ourselves?

As chairman, I invited Dr Andrzej Zurowski, as a representative of the post-Kott generation of Polish critics, to open the discussion.

*

ANDRZEJ ZUROWSKI: Is Shakespeare still our contemporary? No. Shakespeare has sometimes been our contemporary and could be so in future, but only on the condition that he is translated into the questions of our time and takes on the colour of our historical personality.

The Polish dramatist, Stanislaw Wyspianski, said at the turn of the century that the riddle of *Hamlet* in Poland is what it reflects of Poland. The Polish people talk through Shakespeare about their own politics, history, power structures, jobs, orders, and disorders. That is what has happened over the past forty years. We have had more than 450 Shakespearian productions from 1946 to 1986. His plays have been the mirror of our times; and through them we have seen the artistic, but not simply artistic, transformations of our history.

It is not by chance that the concept of the great mechanisms of history came from a Polish critic's pen. Of course, it needed Jan Kott's talent to pick up the vibrations in our society and relate them to Shakespeare. In 1956, the year of Gomulka's *coup d'état*, the riddle of *Hamlet* carried a political message, which Jan Kott formulated in '*Hamlet* after the Twentieth Congress', thus linking it to the return of Gomulka and the end of the Stalinist period.

If we want to say that Shakespeare is our contemporary today, we have to describe how he reflects changes which are happening now; and I would like to compare the two different views of the mechanisms of history expressed by Kott and another great Polish specialist in Shakespeare, Konrad Swinarski. Swinarski was the most outstanding Polish director in the second half of the twentieth century, who tragically died in 1975, just before the premiere of his *Hamlet* at the Stary Theatre in Cracow; and so we have been left with just the notes and recordings of his rehearsals, and a previous version of *Hamlet* which Swinarski directed in 1966 in Tel Aviv.

From those fragments, we can read how one artist nearly twenty years after Kott's essay understood the problem of power in *Hamlet*. Like Kott, Swinarski interpreted Shakespeare through his own experiences, but unlike Kott, Swinarski did not attempt to modernize Shakespeare. Kott had put forward the idea that history repeats itself. He called that the great mechanism. 'History is a circle which returns to its starting point.' Here Kott and Swinarski did not agree. Swinarski thought of history not as a circle, but as an upward-moving spiral.

Swinarski had adopted this idea from the eighteenth-century Italian philosopher, Giambattista Vico, whose theory of the rise and fall of civilizations consisted of three cycles. Each civilization develops an epoch of the Gods, an epoch of heroes, and an epoch of individual people, which is followed by the development of a society. Civilizations may collapse, but as the result of this experience, the next cycle starts at a higher level; and so we find history interpreted as an upward-moving spiral, leading mankind from barbarism to ever higher forms of civilization.

And so, whereas Kott saw the end of *Hamlet* returning to its beginning with the arrival of Fortinbras, Swinarski does not agree; nor does Swinarski quite reflect Vico's point of view. His Fortinbras is more sensible than old Hamlet, better equipped by the intervening experience, but not so wise as the educated Claudius. Whereas the Italian, Vico, was an optimist and saw the upward-moving spiral as an evolutionary process, Swinarski as a Pole saw it more tragically. His Hamlet is a figure filled with pessimism and despair on the eve of brutality's victory. The upward-moving spiral has entrenched the forces of brutality, and has left them better equipped, more perfectly organized.

After the *Hamlet* of 1956, Kott wrote: 'When I looked at the text again, I saw only a drama about political crime.' Twenty years later, Swinarski looked at the sad landscape, with Vico's spiral in his mind, and saw that in Poland time had stopped. For Kott, the tragedy of *Hamlet* was that history was repeating itself, but after all, that is what history in his view always does. It is a circle, which is why Shakespeare is our contemporary. For Swinarski, history ought to move forward and upward. After Vico, after Hegel, history is the movement of structures; but in Poland, it has not moved, only become more entrenched.

Which is right? Kott is right, of course, and, of course, Swinarski is right as well, as were Garrick, Kean and Helena Modjeska. In Shakespeare, everything is told, but nothing is told to the end. Shakespeare is always asking us to give him birth. The riddle of Shakespeare is the riddle of our times. And so Shakespeare isn't our contemporary, but he is waiting for us to make him contemporary, as he has always waited in the past.

A member of the audience immediately replied to Andrzej Zurowski. 'Spiral history is the way in which societies develop through the dialectical

struggle of opposing classes, ideologies and systems. That spiral is the principle contradiction in all our understandings of reality throughout history
and today; and we have to accept that Shakespeare's plays are part of that
spiral. If we start to impose interpretations on Shakespeare, then we lose
his place within history. Throughout this seminar, we have watched the so-
called traditional approach battling with the so-called modern approach;
but both misinterpret history. They really represent opposing political
ideologies of our time, with the conservatives clinging on to an image of
Shakespeare which is "part of our heritage" and therefore should not be
"changed", and the modernists wishing to draw Shakespeare into current
controversies. I would like to draw an analogy here with the way in which
Freud treated Greek drama. Because he came across many examples of
childhood rape and sexual abuse in his clinical work, he started to interpret Greek myths according to that insight; and he propounded his theory
of the Oedipus Complex, in which the story of *Oedipus Rex* was interpreted as an incest myth. But we know that *Oedipus Rex* is actually
concerned with the transition from a matriarchal to a patriarchal society;
and the American feminist anthropologist, Evelyn Reid, has spent seventeen years proving that fact and trying to detach the legend of Oedipus
from Freud's obsession with incest. That is what we have to do with
Shakespeare and all period drama. We have to understand history and the
historical spiral.'

'But can we ever do that?' I asked. 'Can we ever understand history,
whether it's a spiral or not?'

'You're absolutely ignoring', the speaker replied, 'two thousand years of
the tendency struggle in philosophy. You're ignoring the whole struggle
between Marx and the Idealists, who said exactly what you're saying – that
we cannot know what history is about.'

'Well, of course we can't know it absolutely', I said. 'That's clearly
impossible. But you have raised the essential difference of approach
between the purists and the modernists. If we look for what is topical in
Shakespeare, do we also ignore the great differences between his age and
our own? Shakespeare's knowledge and understanding of the world is so
different from ours. Is the world round or not? Does it go round the sun?
His world view is related to the moral order which breathes through his
plays. It is this moral order which we often have difficulty in recognizing
or accepting. If his moral order is essentially different from our own, we
could be limiting the meaning of his plays by simply looking for the topical
connections. But do we have any alternative? Is it really possible to see the
world as he saw it?'

'It can be very dangerous', commented another member of the audience,
'to claim that Shakespeare is our contemporary. It all depends on who is
doing the claiming. Professor Schumacher gave the appalling example of

the way in which the Nazis used *The Merchant of Venice* to stir up hatred against the Jews. Personally, I don't like the way in which Nigel Lawson praised *Coriolanus* and enlisted Shakespeare in his absence as a member of the Tory Party. In the same discussion, Erich Fried said that you can't have great drama in a rotten society. But society is not a coherent group of people who all think the same thoughts. We have many different points of view, as now.'

ERICH FRIED: When I said that you can't have great drama in a rotten society, I should have added 'in the long run', because if a society continues in its rottenness, it will squeeze out the conditions in which people can write and produce great drama. In the short run, of course, a rotten society can provide the provocation for great drama. The contrast between human possibilities and actual human misery can be a spur to great drama.

'Isn't this true of Brecht,' I asked, 'in the early days?'

ERICH FRIED: Yes, but it's complicated. The early Brecht was the Brecht of *Baal*. In *Mahagonny*, which is one of his best early plays, he scathingly criticizes Las Vegas and its values, but he doesn't provide a positive solution. I don't think it is necessary for an artist always to offer a programme for survival. Picasso was asked by a German officer during the occupation of Paris whether he was responsible for those terrible pictures of faces falling to pieces in tears, and Picasso replied, 'No, you are responsible.' To show what is happening is itself an artistic achievement, because you can then leave it to other people's instinct for survival to take steps against the evil thing likely to destroy them.

When *The Merchant of Venice* is so often performed in Israel, it is quite obvious that the play is being used as a partial justification for Zionism, which is quite as much of a distortion of Shakespeare as the Nazis' use of it.

'Shouldn't we distinguish', asked Alfred Emmett, 'between bringing Shakespeare up to date and seeing him as our contemporary? If a director gives a Shakespeare play a particular political slant so that it comments directly on a current event, that is a way of bringing him up to date. But if you approach Shakespeare's plays more open-mindedly, and sincerely try to follow his intentions, then almost inevitably there will be echoes of contemporary life. Michael Bogdanov gave a good example from a

173

production of *Hamlet* where Fortinbras's army goes off to fight for a worthless patch of land, at a time when the Task Force was steaming towards the Falklands. You don't have to stress such connections. You don't have to suggest that Shakespeare was really writing about the Falklands. The connections happen of their own accord.'

ERNST SCHUMACHER: Andrzej Zurowski made the important distinction between Kott and Swinarski, but he forgot to mention that Swinarski was a pupil of Brecht. He may have learnt about the spiral movement of history through Brecht, and how to interpret this mechanism for today. But it's entirely wrong to interpret the great mechanism of history too gloomily. In the darkest tragedies and comedies of Shakespeare, there is always a gleam of hope; and it is this optimistic principle which is of greatest importance today.

Shakespeare lived at a time, as we do now, of grand transformations. He was a contemporary of those who were destroying the Ptolemaic system. He was a contemporary of those who were, for the first time, going round the world; just as we are the contemporaries of those who are going to the moon. We share with Shakespeare that sense of living with a time of fundamental changes.

But it's wrong, in my view, to individualize or to anthropologize our sense of change, to use one man's picture as to what has happened or is happening as a substitute for a more objective approach. We have to combine our knowledge of historical reality with the particular impressions of history from this one witness; and above all, we must remember that it is not possible to find all of our problems expressed through Shakespeare.

'It follows from what Ernst Schumacher has said', I commented, 'that Shakespeare is limited to the problems of his age, as we are limited by ours. By attempting to bridge the gap between these two limited visions, we are perhaps trying to become less limited ourselves.'

'If you go back to look at the historical circumstances in which the plays were written', added a member of the audience, 'you do find these astonishing parallels with today. After seeing John Barton's production of *The Merchant of Venice* at the Warehouse, where the young men on the Rialto were played as irresponsible yuppies, I went back to my history books and found that the Roderigo Lopez affair was engineered by a group of heartless undergraduates, spurred on by the Earl of Essex. Marlowe's comedy, *The Jew of Malta*, wasn't about Roderigo Lopez, because Marlowe was dead before Lopez was arrested; but the Admiral's Men revived *The Jew of Malta* to inflame antisemitism. The Queen rather liked Lopez and didn't want him to be put to death. Shakespeare was not able to write about the situation as he would have liked, because there was censorship and the Earl of Essex was a powerful man. But if you look at Gratiano's horrible remarks during the trial, you will realize that Shakespeare is holding the mirror up to nature in a very brave way indeed. Often when a director and a company of actors go back to the text, and examine the play without any preconceptions, academic or political, then they re-discover the insights of the original, which do indeed seem very modern. And then, as Alfred Emmett said, they can bring out the modernity of Shakespeare without distorting the text. The plays do have to seem modern, because they would have been received in Shakespeare's time as modern plays; and I would like to ask David Thacker whether from his rehearsals for *Julius Caesar*, the play seems as full of contemporary interest as it does to me?'

'Well, we're only at the end of the first week's rehearsal', said David Thacker, 'and at present we feel that Shakespeare is on the side of those who want to get rid of the man who is assuming dictatorial power; but we don't know whether that will be the final analysis. I would like to pick up Erich Fried's point about a rotten society squeezing out great drama. We are alarmed at what is happening in Britain at this moment, with the assaults on the BBC and the introduction of laws which could damage the freedom of the artist. There is this law that has been passed to prevent local authorities from spending money on what are described as political purposes. If somebody protests that our production of *Julius Caesar* is political, presumably our grant from the local authority could be withdrawn.'

'A political point of view', commented Fried, 'is always one which is against the interests of those in power.'

TOBY ROBERTSON: It is obvious, from the way in which we have been talking, that we are always in the process of recreating Shakespeare in our own images. To that extent, he will go on being our contemporary. But I am worried about what is happening to Shakespeare as the poet dramatist. As we talk, form and content are always getting separated.

The history of Shakespearian interpretation by actors has always been a drift towards more naturalism. Thomas Betterton was said to be more naturalistic than Richard Burbage, Quin than Betterton, Garrick than Quin, and so on, to Olivier than Gielgud, and Guinness rather than Olivier. Shakespeare is not just someone who tells a good story. He does, of course, tell good stories, which is why he can translate at all into other languages. But to think of him simply as a storyteller leaves out the poetry.

We in the theatre have a responsibility towards the poetry, but we suffer from a lack of confidence in language. We tend to talk about the literary tradition as if it's something wrong. It is, in fact, a very fine tradition, which persists whether you're doing the play in modern dress or doublet-and-hose. If the language is allowed to express itself, as the violinist has to play the notes, then it succeeds; but often it is not allowed to do that, which is what I mean by the separation of form from content.

'I don't know what you mean', said a teacher in the audience, 'when you say that the language should be allowed to express itself. You can't talk about language as if it were a disembodied entity. Somebody has got to speak it and to put it across to an audience.'

TOBY ROBERTSON: What has happened over the past twenty years is that we have brought the academics into the theatre and we have learnt much more about what the words originally meant. But we have gone so far in the direction of playing for sense, intelligibility and clarity that we have lost the tactile feeling for the words themselves, the assonances and dissonances, the rhymes and half-rhymes. Of course, the language doesn't speak itself, but we have lost the way to speak it. I sometimes think that I don't want to direct Shakespeare ever again, because it will be like working with an orchestra of players who cannot play their instruments.

It goes back to training. We do not train our actors in the classical tradition any longer and so they come to Shakespeare very raw. And there is very little classical work in Britain these days, apart from in the big companies. And so there is no stomping ground where actors can train by trial and error. We are losing the classical tradition and that is, frankly, impoverishing us.

'There is also a trend in the theatre', commented Fried, 'to say that verse should be spoken as if it were prose. T.S. Eliot supported it at one time. I have some theories as to how it came about, but it is obviously wrong.'

RICHARD WILSON: The attack on interpretation and the defence of something called poetry that will speak for itself is based on a complete naivety about language. Language has meaning, because it refers to a social context in which it is spoken. It doesn't speak itself. It has to be constantly re-spoken, re-created in different social contexts.

We should also be aware that every interpretation is, as it were, ideological. Every performance of every production is political in one way or another. There is no innocent inter-pretation. There is no essential Shakespeare who is free from all modern political bias.

Literature, performance, production, what we are doing today, are all interventions in human affairs and in history. Erich Fried has quoted one anecdote of Picasso. I would like to draw your attention to another. As the tanks roared through Paris on their way to the Western Front, Picasso said to Braque, 'We created that.' Every one of us, in the way in which we use language, changes language, and thus intervenes in human affairs. It is naive to suppose that there is some kind of essential language, free from human inter-ference.

ANNA FÖLDES: Yes, of course, every performance interprets and intervenes in history; but I do not like any intervention which does not develop a sense of beauty. I was very pleased to hear what Toby Robertson had to say about the need to bring out the beauty of the language, because interventions are not just ideological but aesthetic as well.

Shakespeare has to be interpreted. I belong to a generation in Hungary which had never seen *The Merchant of Venice* on stage until last season, because we felt that after the holocaust, we could not produce that play. Last year, after a lot of discussion, we decided that it need not necessarily be just a tool for antisemitism but could show how Shylock came to the crime. Shylock was presented as a man isolated from society, insulted and injured, so that the play was against discrimination and against inhuman behaviour on all sides. It was not against the Jew but against all brutality.

'If it is to be performed', said Erich Fried, 'so that the evil is equally shared, then Ernst Schumacher's criticism is fully justified. Shylock has to be shown as a victim of that society, otherwise you start hearing those things that I have heard in Austria, that the blame of Auschwitz lies on both sides.'

'Well, perhaps I am wrong or have expressed myself badly in English', said Anna Földes, 'but the actor who played Shylock was a Jew who had lost his parents in Auschwitz and he did play Shylock as a victim of his society, although Shylock himself also carried a share of the blame. But there is someone else here who saw that production, Carlos Tindemans.'

CARLOS TINDEMANS: I do not know Hungarian and so I was only able to watch the behaviour of the actor on the stage. Two points need to be stressed. The production as a whole was not a good one, but it was saved for me by the performance of this actor, who presented Shylock as someone who desperately wanted to belong within the Venetian society and was not allowed to do so, because he was a Jew. He was also a merchant of money, who wanted to use his money to become accepted or to take his revenge. What was so interesting in the performance was that Shylock had spent his fury before the confrontation with Portia. He knew he had lost, and he was trying for the last time to play weakly according to their rules. One feature unusually stressed in this production was that this was not the final court. Portia was still playing at being a lawyer or a solicitor, unofficially; and so Shylock lost his case before the official verdict came. This man was defeated, as he had been beaten before. But this return to the starting point was not as the result of any great mechanism. There was also a sense of mourning at the end, as the townspeople came back from their festivities. Jessica had already detached herself from society. She stood by herself on the stage, and very slowly, as the sun came up, she started to sing an old Lithuanian song. In that way, it was indicated that others too had tried to belong and been forced back to their true identity.

'What is the great mechanism in *The Merchant of Venice*?' intervened a member of the audience. 'The building of capitalism! Usury on one side and mercantile adventure on the other. Shakespeare is satirizing these two people, Antonio and Shylock. Are they not identical? They're both capitalists and did not the Jew, Shylock, have a function in Elizabethan society?'

DAVID THACKER: There is this strange idea that it is all right for directors to distort or change consciously Shakespeare's meaning for some political purpose; that it's OK if you perform the play like this, but not like that. But that's not what happens.

As an artist, you have to face up to your responsibility to show to an audience what in your view these plays are trying to communicate. If you think that *The Merchant of Venice* is an antisemitic play, the answer is not to change it, but not to do it at all. The same applies to *The Taming of the Shrew*. If you think it's sexist, don't do it.

But if you believe that *The Merchant of Venice* is not a racist play, but shows the source of racism in society, then you can direct the play with a calm conscience. You don't have to show Shylock as a good and pleasant man. He is simply a man, who says, 'Hath not a Jew eyes? hath not a Jew hands, organs, dimensions, senses, affections, passions?' and suffers from the Christians in his society who behave in the most destructive and appalling way. You don't have to alter *The Merchant of Venice* to validate the play, just as you needn't have Katharine slashing her wrists at the end of *The Shrew* to make it less sexist. But if you feel that these plays are sexist or racist, don't do them. There are other plays which you can do instead.

ALEXANDER ANIKST: There are many old habits which it is hard to get rid of. One is the expectation that Shakespeare was a man who, while putting forward a problem, had solved it. That is entirely wrong.

Shakespeare's plays are nearly always problem plays, and not just the ones which we normally call the 'problem plays'. T.S. Eliot called *Hamlet* a 'bad play', because it provides no real answer to anything, not about the hero, not about the political situation, not about anything. And Eliot was in a mood when he wanted answers. He didn't like questions without answers.

But Shakespeare didn't write such plays. He wrote about life with all its complications and problems. Hamlet is not an ideal man and there are critics who will demonstrate that from beginning to end, Hamlet was wrong. Why is this so?

179

It's because Shakespeare was so thorough in describing his characters and in showing the situation from all sides. He saw all sides of the problem. In *Julius Caesar*, Brutus and Cassius are inspired by the noble desire to restore the Roman republic. But what did they bring? Chaos and civil war and eventually dictatorship.

In so many plays of Shakespeare, you find this interesting fact, that people who are good by nature, such as Othello, Hamlet, even Macbeth, blunder all the time. They destroy themselves and those around them. That is a paradox, but it is the paradox of Shakespeare.

Shakespeare, I think, believed that we are cleverer than we really are. He expected us to go away from his plays and think about them, coming to conclusions that can't be expressed in easy formulas. And there was nobody who expressed the problem of *The Merchant of Venice* better than Heinrich Heine, who said, when the play was over, 'By God, the man has been wronged!'

Bernard Shaw was not the first problem dramatist, but Shakespeare. He was the one who wanted us to do our own thinking and he placed some very vital questions before us, generations of critics and actors and directors; and presented us with some very conflicting plots, which we have to understand as best we can.

The worst way of interpreting Shakespeare is to say that he meant this, and just this, and to give a formula. As David Hare said, 'Shakespeare was thinking while he was working through the plot' and this is the right way to approach Shakespeare. He makes us see that this was a tragic fate, or that is a comic fate; and we have to understand what the comedy is, what the tragedy is. But don't ask for simple answers from Shakespeare! Just believe in Shakespeare, in his greatness, in his wide outlook, in his ability to put into one play a whole world with all its contradictions, contrasts and problems.

Alexander Anikst was given so warm a round of applause after this statement and it seemed such an appropriate point on which to close the final session that I was about to do so, when Ernst Schumacher very quietly intervened.

'I don't think you are right', he said. 'Shakespeare does not present all sides to every question in all of his plays. The Christians in *The Merchant of Venice* may be greedy, but Shylock is a usurer, a false tax gatherer, to use the language of the Bible. They may be heartless, but Shylock is pitiless. And they in the end show a kind of mercy to Shylock, which he has refused to show to Antonio. Of course, *The Merchant of Venice* may be interpreted in different ways, but in the end you cannot forget that it has been used down the centuries to stimulate hatred against the Jews. So soon after the holocaust and the murder of six million Jews, it is impossible in my view to play *The Merchant of Venice*. In this respect, Shakespeare is too much of a contemporary.'

'Much as I hate the idea of censorship', said Erich Fried, 'one cannot with an easy mind present *The Merchant of Venice* in Austria or Germany today. I once wrote an epilogue for a production of *The Merchant of Venice* which was given to Launcelot Gobbo, who said, "What a wonderfully civilized approach we have in Venice. We haven't even killed the Jew. We've only taken away his money, his daughter, and his religion. We've only turned him into a Christian, and so we've saved his immortal soul. In our enlightened society, right triumphs over violence." It's very risky to write an epilogue to a Shakespeare play, but I felt that I had to stress the irony for the German audience. I don't think that Shakespeare would have been entirely out of sympathy with this solution.'

'May I summarize?' courteously offered a member of the audience. 'Every Shakespeare text provides a question, to which every Shakespearian production offers a kind of answer. But we can only answer in our own way, using the language that is available to us. The question which puzzles me in *The Merchant of Venice* is the silent man of the title, the merchant himself, Antonio, whom we haven't really talked about at all. In the first session, Erich Fried referred to him as a homosexual and mentioned the delicate way in which the homo-eroticism has been sketched. It had to be delicate because the subject was taboo. W.H. Auden, in his essay *Brothers and Others*, described the parallelism in *The Merchant of Venice* between Shylock and Antonio, and noted that in Dante sodomites and usurers were burnt in the same circle of hell. Six hundred thousand homosexual men also died in the concentration camps with the six million Jews.'

At this point, with *The Merchant of Venice* telling us more about our recent past than we had time to consider, the final session was called to an end.

*

It is a truism to say that absolute communication is impossible, even between two members of the same generation of the same family. Language is a system of socially recognized distinctions, so that if you ask for salt, you are not handed the mustard. You cannot mystically hand over the experience of salt to someone else by simply using that word. Words are only part of the daily language that we use. There are visual symbols as well, such as traffic lights, and myths. They all provide ways in which we can distinguish one experience (or a group of experiences) from another, but they are not identical with the experiences themselves.

It should therefore come as no surprise that Shakespeare's plays can be interpreted in so many different ways and that it is impossible, except in certain limited senses, to assert that one meaning is right and all the others are wrong. But it is an astonishing fact that his plays are still useful to so many people from so many different kinds of cultural backgrounds. Even when we say that Shakespeare thought like this because he was an Elizabethan, we are making a useful distinction between his times and our own, which helps us to get our own lives into perspective.

We knew when we posed the question 'Is Shakespeare still our contemporary?' that there could be no answer, other than the most mundane 'No'. We were looking for a framework within which cultural differences could be sensibly discussed; and we found to our surprise that there was a much greater degree of common understanding than we would have thought possible. Of course, there were profound disagreements between those who thought that Shakespeare was simply a man of his time, and should always be treated as a representative of the Elizabethan age, and those who stressed his 'universality'. Of course, the Brechtians, the Structuralists, the Kottites, the Marxists and the liberals approached Shakespeare from different angles; but we quickly discovered that we were not dealing just with an inkblot, into which anything could be read, but with a more resistant personality, who imposed his own ways of thought to contradict ours, when we became wayward.

In that sense, Shakespeare was our contemporary, helping us to know more about ourselves in our efforts to understand him; and perhaps that is the only way in which any writer can ever be considered a contemporary.

INDICES

INDEX OF CONTRIBUTORS

185

INDEX OF
SHAKESPEARE'S WORKS

GENERAL INDEX

189

191